THE PLACE OF POWER IN YOU

Dear Peyton,

the power of God is in you to fulfill Gods purpose for you life. Keep staying strong!

Blessings,
Toyin John.

THE PLACE OF
POWER IN YOU

TOYIN JOHN

Unless otherwise stated, all Scripture quotations are from the New King James
Version of the Holy Bible.

ISBN: 0996911707
ISBN-13: 9780996911702
Library of Congress Control Number: 2015955532
Published in Irvine, California, by Giant Within Publishing House
Printed in the United States of America.

CONTENTS

DEDICATION

This book is specially dedicated to the One who pulled me out
of the miry clay and set my feet upon the rock to stand –
JESUS CHRIST MY SOLID ROCK..

TESTIMONIALS

Toyin is indeed a Daughter of Destiny! Her book, "The Place of Power in You" is loaded with inspiration for all readers, to inspire us to participate with God as He takes us through the process necessary to prepare us for what He has prepared for us. Read and get inspired as you mature through God's process for your life.

Rev. Kola Ewuosho, Founder
Fountain of Wisdom Ministries International
United Kingdom

The beautiful thing about this book and its author is that, Toyin not only believes in the power of God within us, she lives and walks in it daily. She is a true inspiration of what the power of God can do. What mountain do you need to move?

Missy Day, Founder and CEO
Passion 4Success LLC, Las Vegas, NV

In her book, "The Place of Power in you". Toyin John shares valuable insight uncovering the deception robbing many believers of their God-given power. The truths found in her writing are evident in her own life, a joyous woman of God possessing Christ confidence to overcome any hurdle life places in her path. Your life, like Toyin's, will be transformed with the knowledge and power of who you "truly are" in Christ Jesus. You will never be the same!

Sharon Atkinson, Co-Pastor
New Life Christian Ministries, Roanoke, VA

Toyin John is a woman of true faith and The Place of Power in You is a reflection of her commitment to bringing out the greatness in humanity.

9

Her wise and heartfelt words of paint exquisite pictures of power and her belief in the love and mercy of Jesus Christ. I would recommend this book to anyone who wants to rise above their circumstances and achieve the remarkable.

Guy Dawson, Managing Member
Classy Communications, Las Vegas, NV

Toyin is full of passion and faith. Her strength and confidence come through every word in this book.

Tomas Martinez III, Owner/Publisher
Luxury Home Magazine South, San Antonio, TX

This book is perfect for anyone going through any type of struggle or dark day in life. You'll find scripture-based inspiration to let you know that, you have greatness inside of you and there is more ahead. If you are looking for encouragement, you have found the right book. This is the wakeup call you have been looking for.

Chris Robinson, Owner R3 Coaching,
Founding Member John Maxwell Team

ACKNOWLEDGMENT

A big thank you to my Lord and Savior Jesus Christ, the very reason why this dream has become a reality.

My biological parents, Mr. Odunayo & Mrs Esther Ajayi for always praying for me through thick and thin and especially my mother for instilling great values in me from the start.

My spiritual parents, Rev Kola and Rev Funke Ewuosho for always being there for me through all the years.

My spiritual mother, Rev Funke Ewusoho, for the wonderful impact you've made in my life, words are never enough to express my gratitude.

My ever loving and supportive husband, Dr. Emmanuel Babatunde John, for believing and investing in me. Thanks for allowing a world where I can simply be me and for your never ending love and support.

My lovely children, Tami, Toni and Damilola-Daniel, you are my true gifts.

To my Coach, Guy, for your support, wisdom and insight throughout this process.

To Missy Day, thank you so much for all your support and kindness.

To all my extended family members (Biological & Spiritual) and friends too numerous to mention, who have supported and believed in me through the years, you are highly appreciated.

FOREWORD

THE first time I met Toyin was years ago, when she came to Kano, Nigeria- having just graduated from the University. My husband and I were pastoring the Word of Faith Christian Centre, in Kano at that time. I will never forget the day she walked into my office, and shared a lot about her life with me. At the end of which I said to her, "I believe you are a child of destiny, and I think I can help you." That, indeed, was the beginning of a process.

In her book, Toyin speaks a lot about process. Looking back at her life, from the time I met her, and up till now, I think she is more than qualified to do that. I not only believe she's got something to say on that subject (and all she has endeavored to cover in this book), but I also know she's got a lot to say on it! What gives anyone the authority to say something is the fact that, they practice what they are talking about. Ever since I met Toyin, she has consistently demonstrated (and continues to develop in) many outstanding qualities; which I dare say, are very rare today. Devotion, uprightness, loyalty, consistency, passion, compassion, diligence; to mention a few, are the qualities she has developed over the years. Though Toyin came into our home to help out in the house; as a result of the process God took her through, she became a spiritual daughter, a loyal friend and a confidante! Just like Jesus said to His disciples after a while, "No longer do I call you servants, for a servant does not know what his master is doing; but I have called you friends, for all things that I heard from My Father I have made known to you." (John 15:15 | NKJV).

Toyin has graciously shared the story of her life in this book;

not only the good part of it, but also the bad and the ugly! She has shared the breaking and making of her; even as she still continues to yield herself to be processed the more- knowing that though she has left, she hasn't yet arrived. Just like in the words of Apostle Paul, "I'm not saying that I have this all together, that I have it made. But I am well on my way, reaching out for Christ, who has so wondrously reached out for me." (Philippians 3:12 | MSG).

I recommend this book to everyone, who is looking for a meaning to what they are going through right now in life. I recommend this book to those who want their lives, not only to make a meaning, but also to give a meaning to others.

I believe so much in you and I am extremely proud of you, my dear Toyin. I pray that your hard work be bountifully rewarded, because you deserve the best. Reach beyond the sky; the sky ain't your limits! Well done. I love you lots, Mama Funky's baby girl!

Rev. Funke Ewuosho
Co-Founder, Fountain of Wisdom Ministries
United Kingdom

INTRODUCTION

I must say that, growing up, I loved to read and journal, these two things have always been a part of my life. Reading, especially, created an escape for me; I could go to places in a book and just experience great things. I come from a very humble beginning, what you would call an average family, materially speaking, there was nothing much to show for it. However, I was a raised by a very loving mother who instilled a lot of values in me even before I became a Christ's follower. My father had to live in another city from the time I was nine years old till I turned twenty due to the nature of the work he did at the time so my mom became pretty much both father and mother during that period of my life. She was a no - nonsense woman who had many principles in place that, though it was hard to accept them then but now, my siblings and I are eternally grateful for them. Even though we had discipline and structure we also had love and grew up being very tight-knit and close up to this day.

For my secondary education I went to a boarding school and met quite a number of kids who had come from "rich" homes and that was where for the first time, I saw firsthand that my family had nothing much materially but what we had was more than any material wealth. My experience at this school opened my eyes to a world I did not know existed. I appreciated my mother the more because I could see how she did not allow us to define ourselves by our material or financial status at the time. In her eyes, we had all that we needed for at the time and in that, we were content.

There was no sense of lack in our mentality though we did not have much. This principle has remained with me till today.

I learned a lot from many teachers and school mates at my boarding school much more than they would ever know. I mastered the art of speaking English at this school because it was not my first language at home. Though I had learned how to speak it before I came to the school as a result of reading a lot and the elementary education I received but "living" the English language came as a result of going to this wonderful boarding school for my secondary education. I had such a hunger to learn and perfect the English language more than anyone would ever know about me at the time, I just had a love for it.

I remember a particular incident where, while I was talking to a senior student, I made a grammatical error which was unknown to me until I overheard her talking about it and laughing at me before her friends, when I heard that, I began to figure in my mind what the right word would have been and I corrected myself and just carried on. The senior student went a step further by calling me before her friends and asking me to repeat what I had earlier on said to her, what she did not know was that, I had figured out the right answer and that was what I repeated to her and her friends. The laughter and mockery stopped when I said the correct thing, she told me I was free to go. Honestly speaking, right now, I cannot even remember who the senior student was but I do remember that incident. I was just a twelve year old kid in a boarding school hungry to learn. Since that day up till now, I have never stopped learning from my mistakes or from others. Incidents like that have shaped how I treat others, taught me not to laugh at or mock people in their places of vulnerabilities.

I had an inkling about my future but everything I would go through in between up until recent years did not paint a picture of that future but in retrospect, everything I had been through has prepared me and whatever I go through now continues to prepare me because I have not in any way arrived. In reading this book, I shared about meeting my spiritual mother and how that encounter became the beginning of a phase that has become a major pillar in my life.

In His own infinite mercies, God has sent many wonderful people in to my life to help me on this journey, I have not gotten here all alone, from my biological parents, to my spiritual parents, my husband, spiritual big brothers and sisters, many family members, friends, mentors and colleagues, I have been richly blessed to learn from others and continue to learn from others, my life has been greatly shaped by my encounters and for this, I am forever grateful.

While I do not impose my faith on anyone, I cannot also deny that, without it, it is not likely I would be where I am today, writing this book and doing all the things that I am doing now. What I have with my Lord and Savior is what I call a love relationship, if I end up writing a book about it, if and when you read it, you will understand what I mean. It is from this relationship I draw my strength and wisdom on a daily basis. Without Jesus, I am nothing. It would not be truthful for me to not let you know where my confidence comes from. Sometimes, we are prone to look at people who achieve greatness as people who are somehow "super" in one way or the other but I am just an ordinary person with an extraordinary God who manifests Himself through me as I deliberately and consciously walk with Him and make myself available for His use.

If you consider where I come from, by worldly standards, I should not be where I am today but all my experiences in life and my insight into spiritual things have shown me that, there is a place of power in each and every one of us. God has deposited that power in us so that, we can live a victorious life here on earth. This is what gives life to the giant within us. That giant will go through many processes before it can manifest but it starts with an awareness for every individual to know that, you were made for a purpose, you are not a mistake, regardless of your background and your experiences in life, you were made to carry out an assignment in this life, to glorify God and add value to people. It is your responsibility to discover, work on and use it.

It is my sincere prayer, that this book will bless everyone that reads it, one way or another. There are many stories that will paint vivid pictures in your mind and may be related to what you have gone or may be going through. My joy and fulfillment will be that, God gets the glory and every reader is greatly and positively impacted by the messages shared in this book.

For the glory of God alone, He is worthy!

CHAPTER 1

LIVING FROM THE PLACE OF POWER

POWER means different things to different people, it can be overstated, understated or not even stated at all. Power is simply and basically defined by several dictionaries as "an ability to act." While it has a wide variety of application, the underlying factor is still that; it is an "ability to act or perform."

In the context of this book, the power I am referring to comes from God. When we come to believe in Him, He gives us the right to become His own. **(John 1:12)** What a blessing! The amplified version of the Bible further describes this right as **"authority and privilege."**

What a joy to know that, we are not just existing to deal with life on our own and in our own human ability. The truth of the matter is, our human ability has a limit and it can only take us so far but when we walk in the knowledge of the authority that God has bestowed on us, then, we are connected to a Source that has no limits.

When we operate from the place of power in us, we can move mountains! We can do the impossible! We can live life with a purpose regardless of what is thrown at us.

Talking about power here is knowing that, you are a child of the living God, He lives in you therefore His raw power lives within you. When Jesus Christ came, He took away everything that separated us from God and before He departed from this world, He promised the coming of the Holy Spirit. He told His disciples that;

"But you shall receive power when the Holy Spirit has come upon you." (Acts 1:8).

When that power came upon the followers of Christ and they walked in it, things happened. Simon Peter, who out of fear and cowardice denied Christ three times, received that power and boldness came upon him. He preached openly before thousands of people. The Holy Spirit is the very presence of Christ in us, the power of God at work in our lives.

I truly believe that, the day a Believer of Christ discovers that God's power resides in him or her, that day should be a glorious day. The person should see things differently and respond to situations and circumstances from God's perspective. Living from the place of power is living and breathing from the knowledge of who you are in Christ and exercising dominion over every ability of the enemy.

No power on earth, under the earth or wherever can compare to the power of God living within us. When we walk in the realization of this, we will surely live from a winning standpoint. It does not exempt us from facing challenges in life, Christ said that, in this world, we would face tribulations but He also said, we should be of good cheer because He overcame the world. **(John 16:33)** He deprived it of its power to harm us and conquered it for us. We are victorious through Him! We are winners no matter what life throws at us. Lift up your head and stand up strong! You are an overcomer, head or tail you win because Christ fought the battle and gave you the victory. Claim it because it is already yours!

How can you walk in power when you have no idea that you possess it? Or what if you don't know how to exercise it? The enemy will take advantage of the person who does not know his or her rights. Even if you know your right, many times, he wants to challenge you, he will do anything and everything to shake your faith and make you think that, you have nothing but he is a liar and the father of all lies, the Bible tells us that in **(John 8:44)**. When you let him know that you know what rightfully belongs to you, if you hold your position long enough, he has no choice than to surrender.

I shared a story of God's deliverance in a chapter of this book about conquering fear and anxiety, it is my personal story of how through the power of God I overcame. I experienced firsthand how to be free and live victoriously through the ability of God's word. The pathetic thing is that, I had this power within me all the while but then, I unconsciously allowed the enemy to keep me in that bondage. I wonder how many of God's children are currently living in the same situation I was in at that time?

By the power of God, you can get rid of fear, anxiety, worry, mediocrity, low thinking, defeatism and so on and so forth. These are not God's plan for His children, they are lies that come on as a result of many things that we experience and go through in life. We live in a broken world that constantly challenges our identity. Every situation is asking us a question. Who do you believe in? Who are you? What are you going to do now? Where do you go from here? Take a moment to think about this, every situation is asking you and me a question.

For those who believe in God, those questions come to challenge our identity. The first time I heard this, was years ago being

taught by my spiritual father, a light came on within me! I saw the
enemy of our souls for who he truly was. When the Lord Jesus
Christ was tempted by the enemy, His identity was being challenged. The devil says; "if You are the Son of God, command that
these stones become bread." **(Matthew 4:3)** What if the Lord
Jesus did not know who He was? What if He was not aware of
what was already His?

This is the same tactic that, the enemy through various situations, trials and tribulations of life tries to do to a believer, that
is; challenge your identity. When you know who you truly are, you
can operate from that reality.

Imagine a soldier sent into the battlefield without any armor
to protect him against the attacks of his opponents or weapons
to defend himself? That soldier will be a "toast" for his enemy.
It is sad to say that, many Christians are a "toast" for the enemy
not because they do not have the armor to protect them or the
weapon to fight with but because they do not wear their armor
nor do they use their weapon. What is the use of the power you
possess and do not utilize? Go figure! The devil knows this and
he is taking advantage of many Believers. The word of God is our
weapon and it creates a protective shield for us when we rightly
divide it. He has made everything we would ever need available
through His word. You and I must spend time in His word, we
must constantly create the time to know God intimately through
fellowshipping with Him. Our eyes will be open, our vision will be
clearer and when circumstances of life come challenging us, we
will know exactly how to combat them.

I want to stir up a holy anger within you with every chapter of
this book, rise up and take your place in God, rise up and exercise
that power in you. You are the child of the living God! The Maker
of heaven and earth is your Daddy! Everything He has, you own,

no force on this earth can overcome a child of God who knows his or her right and exercises it. You do not have to beg God for that power, it is already in you, it has been given to you when you received Christ and placed your trust in Him. Yes, you will face battles, you may even get hit sometimes, things may be thrown at you but remember you are already more than a Conqueror through Jesus Christ who loved you! **(Romans 8:37)**

For someone who is not a Believer, you cannot really claim this right my friend, even though God loves you, knowing about God and actually having a relationship with Him are two different things. Having a real relationship with God starts with acknowledging that, you are a sinner, believing that God sent Christ to save you, confessing your sin and declaring Christ as your personal Lord and Savior. The Bible says, with the heart man believes unto righteousness and with the mouth confession is made unto salvation. **(Romans 10:10)** If you fall into this category, do not waste any more time, do this now, surrender your life to God, you will receive the right to become His very own and have access to the power and authority that only His children have.

To live victoriously in this life is to be able to access the power of God in you. A place where you know who you are, take your stand against every wile of the enemy and enjoy the full life that God intends for you to live but remember, getting to know God intimately and having His word come alive in you are two things that will activate that power in you!

CHAPTER 2

YOU ARE NOT YOUR CIRCUMSTANCES

M ANY people had it really good, in that, they were born into a life of comfort and luxury, a life where there was no lack and little challenges. To many of these people, they may be an envy of their peers and sometimes, their affluent status alone makes life seem unfair to others though they have nothing to do with it.

On the other hand, some people had it tough; many were born into difficult and sometimes hopeless situations. I have heard stories of people growing up in unbelievable circumstances, sometimes to have one meal a day was a luxury. Many went without food, many lived in pitiful and unstable environments.

Some other people regardless of what their background was have been through some tough and sad circumstances in life that have left them damaged and broken on the inside, sometimes, the effects of these brokenness and damage affect everything in their lives and their perspective about life.

You might have been born into a wealthy family, do not rest on the laurels of that affluence, instead, discover who you are and make your own footprints in this world. You might also have been born into very difficult situations, do not allow this to chart the course of your life in a negative way because that will probably repeat the cycle.

Life might have treated you badly and unfairly and this might have left you bitter and angry thus blurring your vision of living a victorious life. You must realize that, you are not your circumstances. You are not the difficult situations you were born into or that you experienced. If you would not make them a crutch but rather allow them to work for you, it will amaze you the qualities that will come forth from you. I truly believe that, when we allow God to work through our circumstances, great things will happen.

We live in a world where people define us many times according to what they know about us or fame, status and material possession rather than appreciating us for who we truly are. The truth is that, we do not have a control over how people define us but we do have a control over how we let it affect us or how we respond to it.

I am fully persuaded that, how we do not let it affect us is by looking inward and knowing within ourselves who we truly are, realizing that, we matter, we have something to bring to the table. By seeing with an inner vision that, because we were made in the image of God, we have greatness within us and because of this, we have a lot to offer humanity and if we allow God in our lives, He will work wonders through us.

The realization of this alone can turn on a light within us to begin an adventure of discovering the purpose for which we were made. Once we discover that purpose, we can begin working on ourselves to be the best we can be and be true to our God given assignments in life.

It is important to know that, discovering that purpose alone will not get us to our destination but working on it, developing ourselves constantly by being students of life and connecting with the Giver of these abilities who is the Creator God will get us there.

It does not even matter right now what your circumstances are or what situations surrounded your birth and upbringing, if you don't let them define you, you can arrive at a most wonderful place far better than where you started no matter how good or how bad it was.

I am reminded of the story of a man called Les Brown, who was born in an abandoned building and given up for adoption along with his twin brother at six weeks old. He was adopted by a woman who had a big heart but little financial ability to raise them in abundance. They lived in the poor section of the city and his adopted mother worked in the school cafeteria and as a domestic worker for a rich family. Academically, Les did not perform well in school, he was declared as educably mentally retarded and got held back as a result of this. He was mocked by others at school and called 'DT' meaning, the 'dumb twin'. Many did not believe in him, they saw no good in him.

Destiny has a way of setting us up, Les had an encounter with a teacher who spoke life into him and challenged him never to allow someone else's opinion become his reality. This ignited a fire within him that could not be quenched and the person that had all these odds against him is one of the leading motivational speakers in the world today.

How many people are out there today who have many odds stacked against them and they have bought into that and allowed those circumstances to define them? There are others who cannot look past the fact that, they were born into unfortunate circumstances and have accepted that, it would remain their lot in life. They have no zeal for life in any form or fashion talk less of fulfilling purpose.

It does not matter what your story is, you have the power in you to not allow any negative history define you. You may not have a teacher like Les Brown did, one who can challenge your thinking and breathe belief into you but God is sending this book your way to let you know that, He did not make a nobody and you are not your circumstances. Whatever you might have gone through in life can really work for your good. It can make you a stronger person emotionally and psychologically, you may become more compassionate and empathetic towards others but all these things are not automatic, it depends on how you allow those circumstances to affect you.

Joyce Meyer is a great woman of God, affecting the lives of millions today both men and women. You may look at her life now and you see the huge platform, the spotlight, the big crowds and the big ministry. The truth of the matter is, she did not start out like that. When you look at everything that surrounded her upbringing, in the natural, it is almost impossible to even begin to visualize how she could have mentally survived all those things talk less of being used by God today to bring healing and deliverance to many.

She gives her testimony from time to time in her speeches; having being raised by an abusive and angry father who sexually molested her for many years and a mother who was too weak to do anything about the situation. Joyce's childhood was a very miserable and an unhappy one and all these unfolding events in her life had a negative impact on her for a long time.

When you see or hear her or read one of her books today, it shows the redeeming power of Jesus Christ that is able to turn a mess into a message, a trial into a triumph and a test into a testimony. As a result of her surrendering her life to Jesus Christ and allowing Him to work through her, she has healed in an unimaginable way and she has been transformed enough to help others. In spite of this painful ordeal, she was able to forgive her parents and even witnessed her father's salvation before he died. Yes, her transformation did not happen overnight but she is an excellent example of how God can bring a powerful message out of a mess.

The problem with a lot of people is that, they let their circumstances make up the total sum of their lives. When you look at it closely, such a person is already defeated, they may be alive, going through the motion like many other people but they are not victorious. You cannot go past the vision you see for yourself. If the vision is twisted, then life is twisted, you are not expecting much to come out of it.

Whatever you might have gone through may be a reality but it does not have to be the navigation system that dictates the rest of the course of your life. Like Joyce Meyer, things can turn around for you completely that when you tell your story, people will find it almost unbelievable because of the change that will take place.

In order for situations to change on the outside, a conversation of change must begin on the inside, things just don't happen automatically, there is a responsibility that an individual has in causing change to happen. The good news is that, if everyone seeking a change in their circumstances will tap into the abundant grace of God, the journey to victory will be a fruitful one and they will never be alone.

Here are some helpful steps that can help you;

DELETE:
There must be a change of mindset! If peradventure, you have consciously or unconsciously allowed your circumstances to define you, there must be an immediate

rejection of that lie because you are not your circumstances. You must begin to get rid of every lie that the
enemy has sown in your heart as a result of what you
have been through. Press the delete button in your mind
and flush those lies out. Pull down those strongholds for
they are a hideout for satan. *(2Corinthians 10:4-6)*

UPLOAD:

This is the process of renewing the mind, you can't leave
the house of your mind empty, and there is no more
powerful way to do this, than to believe what God says
about you. Study scriptures that talk about the promises
of God regarding you, declare them constantly, repro-
gram your mind with them, meditate on them and your
heart will catch on. *"For as he thinks in his heart, so
is he." (Proverbs 23:7)* Upload the files of God's word
into the system of your heart.

ACTIVATE:

Let your words match your action. Talk like a winner,
behave like a victorious person, do things like an overcomer. Embrace a new identity in what God has called
you not what situations have called you. His word says,
**"you are fearfully and wonderfully made." *(Psalm
139:14) "He has your name engraved on the palm of
His hands." (Isaiah 49:16)*** You are made in His image!
What a blessing. You are God's creation and He is your
inheritance. Call yourself what He calls you and answer
only to that. Walk in it completely and let His power be
activated within you.

I must warn you that, this is not just a 3 step help you do once and you live happily ever after. The enemy of your soul will come to challenge your new walk every now and then to see if you are firmly rooted, you can't afford to be passive, he's a dirty fighter so put up a fight within you to live the life of an overcomer. Don't allow the negative things you have thrown out to come back again. Hold on to the truth you now know with all tenacity and constantly walk in your freedom.

CHAPTER 3

RISE UP FROM THE ASHES

IT is true that sometimes life is not fair, when you look at what happens to someone and what they have had to endure or overcome, you wonder why life deals such hard blows on people sometimes.

One thing I have found out though, is that, God in His infinite mercies helps us through difficult times if we will embrace His help. He has deposited a strength within us that can overcome insurmountable circumstances.

If you are going through anything today, you must be able to open your mind to know that, there is a light at the end of the tunnel and if you won't give up, you will surely overcome. It has often been said that, the fact that you fail does not mean you are a failure. Just because you suffered a setback does not mean you are a failure. I think that is very powerful, it is easy to throw in the towel and lift your hands up in surrender and say, "I give up". This does not bring any solution when you really think of it. There is no hope in nothingness, there is no victory in quitting and there is no joy in surrendering to defeat.

I remember starting a new business and not knowing how to deal with the rejection that goes along with the territory of sales. I had been hurt many times in my life that, I had learned to build a thick wall around me so that, no one could penetrate in to hurt me anymore. This attitude does not grow us, I must quickly add, it sometimes makes us to shut off from many opportunities that God may bring our way in life. The business I got involved with entailed that; I must approach strangers and get familiar with them enough to present my products. Due to the fact that, I started the business not knowing anyone, it became mandatory for me to reach out to the people I did not know. The experience was so excruciating at first because the very mention of 'NO' from someone sent invisible daggers to my heart. I was exposed to hurt, my walls of 'protection' came crashing down.

I wanted to run, I wanted to quit, I wanted to surrender in defeat but I kept pushing through. I believe in Jesus Christ and what the scriptures say, one of my favorites of all times is in **Philippians 4:13** that says; *"I can do all things through Christ who strengthens me."* I remember declaring this scripture over and over again and when it looked like I had used up all the strength in me, a new wave of strength would just burst forth from the depth of my very being, I knew that was the power of God at work in me.

I kept reaching out to strangers, I got many no(s) but I began to get many yeses too and before I knew it, no(s) no longer had any power over me, I no longer hurt when someone said it regardless of the attitude they had. I had conquered and I began to flourish, not because the whole world began to say yes but because I had grown through these situations and I could handle life better. This very situation spilled over to every area in my life, I was no longer sensitive to things like I used to and I began to handle disappointments, rejections, maltreatments and negativity better.

What am I saying here? Even in the midst of ugliness can arise something very beautiful that can shape our lives for the better.

If I had given up when it hurt so badly, I would not be telling this story today and I would not be the better person for it. I am grateful for the ability in God to be able to rise from those ashes and it has brought tremendous healing to my soul. Little did I know that, God was also going to use that business to train me in so many ways but if I had thrown in the towel at the beginning, I would have missed out on a lot of growth that I gained from being in that circle.

Whatever your own "ashes" may be, I want you to know that, you can rise up from those situations. I had to lean on and draw strength from God because as a human being, our strength has limits before we crumble under pressure. It is amazing to know that, His strength starts where ours ends. The beautiful thing is that, He is ready to make it available to anyone who would come to Him.

Don't allow circumstances to back you up in a corner; that is a helpless position. You deserve to live your life to the fullest. You can take charge of anything that comes into your mind and goes out through your mouth. You can take charge of your thoughts and decide what you will allow to dominate you. You can refuse to go down in defeat and fight back, you can decide to get up from the ashes and awaken to a newness of life. Every ability, every power to do that has been given to you by God. All you have to do is realize it, dig deep within you and fetch it out.

It is possible that, you may have gone through so many horrible situations in life, people might have treated you badly and life might not have seemed fair, yet, I know that, you can still rise up from the effects of those circumstances and end up living a victorious life. You may be debating in your mind how that is even possible but it is. With God, all things are possible and to him that believes, all things are possible, *(Matthew 19:26; Mark 9:23).*

You must accept that, God does not take any pride in seeing His
creation defeated, weak and beaten by the enemy, that does not
bring Him any joy. I know that, when we turn over the broken
pieces of our lives to Him, He can mold something great out of
them. He can turn a mess into a message of victory.

I believe that, we came from God, we were made in His image
the Bible says, which means that, He is our Source but it is sad to
say that, many people are trying to live life disconnected from the
Source of life Himself. While this can work for some time, on the
long run, there is no eternal value in it. If you want to iron a piece
of clothing, you have to connect the plug into the socket so that,
there can be a transmission of power into the iron. Only then, will
the heat come into the iron. Likewise, if we as human beings are
not connected to the Source of power which is God Himself, how
can we live life as overcomers?

It is a great privilege to have a personal relationship with God,
I am not talking about organized religion, rules of legalism and
things of that nature but knowing God in a personal relational
way, where you talk to Him as a Father, a Daddy, a Friend, only
then can you experience Him in a way too marvelous for words.

A lot of people are sitting in their ashes having a limited vision
of their future but if only they knew how much God loves them
and how much He longs to step in and help them, they would not
waste one more minute in the ashes.

The ability to rise from the mess of life is within us, it is the
power of God Himself. It will turn your life around if you allow
Him to. Everything you've been through will work for your good,
that is the promise of God but you must let Him in, and if you
have let Him in, you must open your heart and let Him pick you
up.

CHAPTER 4

STAND UP AGAINST MEDIOCRITY

A mediocre life is a life that thinks averagely, poorly and accepts anything and everything that comes as though that is how it should always be. A mediocre person never goes against the grain, resists change and cannot accept life outside of his or her comfort zone. The giant within a mediocre person is locked in a prison and though constantly crying for help to be released cannot be heard because mediocrity does not see beyond the present. Any attempt to see far is too painful, too uncomfortable, so it is always better not to rock the boat of comfort in the territory of mediocrity.

The truth is that, every person who must be what they have been created to be must fight against mediocrity at some point in life. There may be many falls, tears, bruises, wounds and heartbreaks along the way but the fight against mediocrity is a real fight but gladly it is a fight that can be won.

Someone said, God did not create "nobodies" He created every person for a unique purpose but it is our responsibility to discover that purpose and use it to His glory and the benefit of humankind. Circumstances and issues of life can sometimes blind people's vision from seeing that, they have been created for greatness. Due to this, they just go through the motion and live life as it comes.

I once heard a saying that made much sense to me, that; "when a person discovers the purpose they have been created for, then, and only then do they start living." Do you know why you are here? Are you living your life for that very purpose or have you accepted things the way they are and just coasting along?

I believe that, when you truly discover why God has put you on this earth, you will not live a minute with mediocrity any longer. You will send it packing and you will strive towards living life with a purpose and showing others the way.

Standing up against mediocrity has nothing to do with having more money although, that can happen, it starts with changing the way you think about yourself and the way you see things.

If you were born into a poor family and had nothing much going on for you while you were growing up, worse even, the atmosphere you were born in to might have been a very negative one, it is natural for you to see life the same way if you do not open your mind to the possibilities that abound outside of your circumstances.

You must first of all, accept in your thinking that, though, your upbringing might have been very unglamorous but that does not mean it should dictate the rest of your life. Once that is settled in your mind, you may want to look at the opportunities that are out there that can help you in your quest. Getting a good education might be one, surrounding yourself with positive thinking, successful people is another one. Laying hold on resources that can help you upgrade your thinking is a very good one. Being accountable to at least one person who loves you unconditionally but can also tell you the truth constructively is a major one. Living a life of excellence, applying discipline and hard work is key to standing against mediocrity. This is just one example and there are many more.

Let's look at the true story of a man called Noel, who was born into an average family, but that average quickly went down to nothing. Hard times hit, his father lost his business and eating at least one meal a day became a luxury for the entire family. The standard of living for them was pitiful because his parents could not provide much for them. Though the father found another job, it paid so little and could do nothing for the family. Many times, they were at the mercies of others for daily sustenance.

Right from when Noel was young, he had always dreamt about being great. He found solace in his faith and quickly developed a relationship with God. He strove hard to excel in his academics, he saw education as a ticket out of poverty and mediocrity. In his country, education is highly esteemed so he made it his life's goal to go as far as he could. He found love in learning and teaching others. He faced many challenges along the way but he kept on forging ahead and kept on looking forward to a brighter future. It took him many years but today, he is a huge success in his own right. He is living excellently well and he is impacting the lives of many in his circle of influence. If you look at where he is now and compare it to the unbelievable circumstances he came from, you would know that, he is a man who has had to fight hard against mediocrity in his life.

In Noel's case, he acknowledged that, he had to change his mindset from what he was used to, he had to replace many pictures in his heart that mirrored hopelessness with the ones that brought hope and light to the darkness of his situation.

He placed his faith in Jesus Christ and began a relationship with him that totally transformed his life. He surrounded himself with mentors that pointed him in the right direction. Since the major thing that plagued his family was poverty, it was natural for him to seek what God's word says about that. He discovered so many scriptures that speak of a God who provides for His own and actually takes pleasure when they prosper. He began to apply this into his thinking pattern while working hard on the outside to develop himself career wise. These were the instruments that he used to change his mind set and his life.

The moral of Noel's story is that, even though he was raised in abject lack and sympathetic situation but he concluded that, it did not have to be the natural course of his own life too. He made a detour when he began to change his thinking pattern with the word of God after having placed his faith in Christ and discovering his identity in Him.

The fact that, someone places their trust in Jesus does not mean that, things will automatically change, there is still work to be done. Standing up against mediocrity is first of all fighting against every thought that challenges who God says you are in your mind.

You can have what God says you can have, you can do what God says you can do. Every dream within your heart, if in line with God's purpose for your life can come to pass, if you first of all believe it and go to work to do your part.

It has been said that, the battlefield is in the mind. Sometimes, if you are not careful and you play with a lie for so long, it can become your truth and shape your thinking or the way you see and respond to things.

Our mind must be renewed. The best resource for me has always been the Bible, there, I see who God says I am and what He says are mine and I am able to make informed decisions to change my thinking from that standpoint and this has become my reality. I see in it that, He is a God of excellence not a mediocre God, that challenges me to want to be the best that I can be and not settle for less than God's best since He lives in me.

You have to go at life actively because if you are passive in your response to it, you may just pass through it and live life as a mediocre. Life is constantly moving, changing and rocking, you can't afford to be passive.

Mediocrity loves complacency, it does not like to challenge anything and finds solace in comfort zones. Making extra effort is too painful to a mediocre person and striving to do better is completely out of the equation. In the land of mediocrity, giants stay asleep and even when they are roused up from their sleep, they wobble and wobble without trying to get up till they sink back down into a deep slumber.

When we know how much of the power of God is deposited in us, we will strive for excellence because He is an excellent God. Every human being has a piece of the Almighty within them, that is what responds when God comes calling, whether they believe in Him or not, that is the power that sets the creation of many things into motion. Whether we will use it for His glory or not is a different matter. The knowledge of the fact that, He is the Almighty, we were created in His image,   after His likeness is enough for anyone to rise up and kick mediocrity in the face.

There is more that is within us that is yet to be discovered than what we are manifesting, there are songs not yet sung, many poems not yet written, many inventions not yet discovered, my favorite book says*, "Eye has not seen, nor ear heard , nor have entered into the heart of man, the things which God has prepared for those who love Him" (1Corinthians 2:9).* Thank God for the sweet by and by but here in this life, we are to live life to the fullest according to God's plan, purpose and design and that has nothing to do with mediocrity.

CHAPTER 5

PROCESS DOES NOT HAPPEN OVERNIGHT

I T is possible to see far into the future and catch a glimpse of greatness, I believe that, it is a divine ability that allows one to do that. However, you may catch a glimpse of a wonderful future and your present situation may be remotely connected to it. It takes a process for a little boy to grow into a man. That process cannot be skipped, it must take its full effect in order for a healthy and sound grown person to emerge. Many times, the process will have some "growing pains" but it is all part of the total picture.

A young man named Joseph in the Bible had a dream about a wonderful future, where he was in charge and everyone paid obeisance to him as a result of his position. He was so confident that he bragged about his dream to his brothers who already hated his guts in the first place. He also told his father who, though loved him, rebuked him and still marveled at the concept of that dream. He had the dream when he was only seventeen years old, little did he know that, the next thirteen years of his life would prepare him for when that dream would become a reality. He went through a process he did not foresee, a journey he did not expect nor wish for.

He was thrown into a pit by his jealous brothers and later sold as a slave into a strange land, far away from the love of his father

and the comfort of his home. I truly believe that, he had a relationship with God and leaned on Him when times were tough for
him. Due to this, the grace of God was evident in his life and in
all that he did. His master made him an overseer of his household
and he was put in charge. He conducted himself well and took
great care of his master's affairs.

I would have to pause and deviate a little bit, when you know
the lineage of Joseph in the Bible, it is a lineage with a great heri-
tage, Joseph had every right to be depressed for being sold as a
slave, he could have been angry and bitter at how unfairly he was
treated but if he had given in to these negative emotions, how
would he have been able to exhibit that spirit of excellence that
made his master take note of him? How would the grace of God
have flowed freely through him so evident that others saw it?

Along the line, even his relationship with God was tested,
his master's wife began to lust after him to the point of literally
tempting him to commit immorality with her, he being a God
fearing man, refused, declaring that he would not sin against God
and fled the scene of the temptation. One would have thought
that, heaven would come to His rescue and vindicate him but no,
his process was not completed yet. His master's wife lied against
him, the master that once trusted him took sides with his wife and
condemned Joseph to a life in the prison.

At this point, he could have pointed an accusing finger at God
and scream why? After all, he honored God through his decision
and did not fall for that temptation and yet he got punished for
what he did not do. But Joseph kept his cool, he kept on trusting
God because again the grace of God was at work in his life. While
he was in the prison, the guard noticed and put him in charge
again! Joseph continued to allow the spirit of excellence to flow
through him. By now, he was a humble man, he had compassion

for others and was genuinely interested in what they were going through. There was no bragging about the "dream" he once saw as a young boy, he was a fully grown man who had gone through the process and attained maturity.

God did not forget him in that prison either because He was the one that gave him that dream in the first place. He allowed the process that Joseph went through and when it was time in God's eyes and Joseph was ready, God orchestrated situations that took Joseph straight from the prison to the position of the number two man in the entire kingdom of a strange land where he was once a slave and a prisoner. What an ending! *(Genesis 39, 40, 41)*

I love the story of Joseph because it is a story that many of us can relate to in our lives. I am sure that, if we study it closely, there are many parallels that we can draw with his process and many lessons we can learn pertaining to how he handled difficult situations in his life.

Joseph could have aborted the plan of God for his life by going against everything he knew to be right in God. He could be bitter and angry thus opening the doors to other negative influences to gain access into his life. He could have easily edged God out of the whole equation and there would have been no way the grace of God would have flowed through him to the point that, people around him were positively affected by it. By the time he went through his process, he was ready for the dream he once saw to come to pass and he was able to be used by God for His glory and the benefit of mankind.

You may have a caught a glimpse into your future or simply have a conversation going on within you that, there is more to life than where you are right now and what you are doing. It may even be that, you have sensed a calling of some sort in your life and you know that, it is bigger than you, it is not what you just came up with rather it is a pull so compelling that you know beyond any shadow of doubt that, you were put on this earth to carry out that assignment. Where you are right now may be so far away from where you believe you ought to be but I encourage you not to take shortcuts.

Go through your process, no matter how hard and difficult it may be sometimes. There will be times when you will be the only one that will believe in you and the calling you may have, it is completely okay. Remember, your particular assignment was given to you and not others, don't be bitter and offended when they don't see it with you. Stay focused on the path that you must take to get you to where you are going. That path will be rough many times, it will be crooked and you may fall sometimes but get back up again, don't stay down.

It is my personal belief that, when you go through your process with God as your Guardian and Helper, the process may not be easy but you will be okay. He will watch over you and cover your back, He will defend and protect you. There may be times when it will look as if, He's gone on a break on you but no, He hasn't, He is right there every step of the way. Remember, when a piece of diamond is first found, it is a piece of dirty muddy rock until it goes through a process and comes forth as what is so valuable. It is the same with us too. As human beings with carnal nature, our character must be developed so that, we are able to carry out our assignments with little or no problem. Many people want to be leaders today without first of all learning how to follow. How can you give what you don't have?

There is a lot of dying to self that will take place when you go through the process, many things about you will be exposed not to shame you but to allow you to deal with them so that, they no longer have control over you. God may place people in your life that will confront issues about you that, ordinarily you'd rather not go there but if you submit yourself to the process, you will come out better and well equipped and able to help others.

As a teenager who had given her life to Christ, I had an inkling that, I was going to be used by God and America was going to be my mission field. I had no idea how it would come to pass because there was nothing in my background that was connected or headed towards that direction. It was strongly impressed upon my heart and it also came with a "knowing" within me that it would eventually come to pass. It was just there and never left me. Everyone that came close to me enough knew I carried that in my heart. It was undeniably present in my being so clearly I knew that somehow, some way, it would be done, I just did not know how.

As time went by, in my own way, I tried to plan things the best I knew, now when I look back, I can say that, I was trying to help God bring this promise to pass. Nothing worked until I completely surrendered. Where I was taken next was a complete surprise to me and everyone in my life at the time. I thought I was supposed to be heading to America to fulfill the "call" but God had something else in mind.

I had finished a four year university program and was at a crossroad. It was in the midst of this I became involved with a church and I believe up to this day, that I perceived in my heart that, the Lord asked me to go and submit myself to the woman of God (who later became my spiritual mother) and serve her. She was my lady Pastor at the time. When I first met her and told her my story, she looked at me and affirmed that I was a child of destiny. That was the first time, someone acknowledged a knowing I had carried within me for years. It was natural for me to be drawn to her because she said she would help me in my journey. She must have seen some things in my life that needed work.

Little did I know that, I was about to go through a real life transformation process. I began to live with her and her family in order to serve and so many things happened as a result of living in that home that contributed to how I have turned out in life. My character went through a major development. At the time, though I loved Jesus, I was like an untamed horse in my attitude and actions. I was so immature as a Believer and reacted negatively and immaturely to many situations. I let my emotions run the show many times. If I did not like something, it was not long before you knew it because it was written all over my face. I gave a piece of my mind "undiluted" all the time to people, it was not a pretty situation. How could God have used me in that state? I have a huge respect in my heart till this day for all the people in my life that put up with me during all those years.

It is important to say that, when I heeded the call to submit and serve, it was not to assist to preach or sing or do anything out front, it was to stay in the house tending to their three little kids, keeping the house and attending to the needs of the man and woman of God. In the culture I grew up in, when you graduate from the university and serve the government for a year, you go and get a job. As for me, there was a prospect of a bank job waiting for me that was truly promising due to certain connections. Working in the bank was a big deal in my community at the time. When I said no to this and decided to "serve" my Pastors, I came against some oppositions and mockery. It is easier for me to talk about them now but back then it was really tough, it took every ounce of grace to keep it together sometimes.

You see, it was easy for people to look at things from the outside and see me helping them because I took care of those three little kids and kept the house but in the true sense of it, I was the one who needed help, I was the gold that needed to go through the refiner's fire, I was the one that was truly being helped. This is one of the reasons why the story of Joseph is so personal to me, I get it. *Job 23:10 says; "But He knows the way that I take; when He has tested me, I will come forth as gold".*

In the midst of it all, God was preparing me, shaping me, molding my character, using the man and the woman of God to help me in many ways. I must admit that, many times, the "help" was not funny, comfortable or easy but God began to use all these to take layers and layers of flaws off of me. When things you have been used to, that have become a part of you are being confronted, believe me, it is not fun. But God knew what I needed and He sent me to the right place and I was there for almost seven years going through this process.

I was discipled by watching how they lived their lives as Christians behind the scenes in their home. I saw firsthand how one could literally depend on the word of God and experience some manifestations. It was a faith building journey. I caught so many things while living with them that, well over a decade later after having left to start my own family, I am still living by many of those principles. Today, these man and woman of God are spiritual parents to my husband and me. They have been instrumental in our lives in so many ways.

God could not use me untamed, wild, insecure and immature at the capacity He would want to even though I loved Jesus, I had to go through my process of breaking, molding and shaping. I have heard many times that, your "anointing will take you to the top but it is your character that will keep you there". Another one says, "What you don't deal with will eventually deal with you". Looking back now, that period of my life has become a huge highlight because it was a major character formation period for me. Though my character is still being formed everyday as I walk closely with Jesus, dying to the flesh is a daily thing for me now but that period with my spiritual parents was undeniably a very monumental one in my life.

God, at the tail end of my stay with them, brought the man who became my husband into my life, opened the door for both of us to come to America and the rest is history. He has been using me in different capacity to touch people's lives since I came to the US but He did not send me here unprepared. What God said and what He showed me when I was a teenager, He Himself is bringing to pass effortlessly and continues to unwrap His plans as years go by. Everything that did not make much sense then makes sense now and if I can sum it all up in one sentence, I would say, He has been taking me through a process the whole time, preparing me for what He has prepared for me.

I don't know the dreams in your heart or the glimpses of greatness that, God has shown you in times past, I encourage you to be true to your process, sometimes, when you follow His leading, it may not make sense to you yourself or anyone that knows you but if you feel in your heart that, God is leading you in the right direction, follow His lead because He never makes mistakes. Don't try to run away from your process because it may delay your journey to the Promised Land.

Joseph did not run away from Potiphar's house, rather he stayed there and became the best he could be, cooperating with the process that God was working out in his life. He did not try to break out of the prison and escape, he cared for others until the day of his visitation from God came. I believe he must have trusted God, he must have had a full assurance in his heart that, what He promised, He would do.

A friend once told me when I was at that crossroad and was wondering what I was supposed to do next, she said, "the time of preparation is never wasted". This statement stuck with me through the years and many stages of life, now I appreciate that statement more than ever before because looking back at how far God has brought me, I can see the hand of God evident in every aspect all the while.

I give you the same encouragement, God will prepare you before He launches you, it may come at different times for different stages of His plan for you but the time of preparation is never wasted.

There is a peace that can flood one's soul even in the midst of tough situations, it is a force that cannot be explained in ordinary terms. I believe that Joseph had that peace which was why he was able to focus on what he was doing at Potiphar's house and the prison. I know what that peace means because I had it, when the situation I was in did not look like the promises I had been given by God, when oppositions of different sort rose up against me, the peace of God was the umpire for my soul, it kept me focused and brought me through.

For the giant within you to rise up, the proper process must take place, character must be developed so that you are able to walk in the fullness of God's plan and purpose for your life. Submit yourself to your process, whatever that might be to you. Be open and attentive to the spirit of God and He will lead you.

If you are already in a process, trust God and stick with it, you have the divine power within you to get through with it. God has placed that ability in each and every one of us to help us in our journey through life.

The fact that, I went through one process does not mean that was all the process I would need to go through. At different stages in life, different processes continue to emerge but the beautiful thing is that, He brought me through one, He is able to bring me through many other ones, I can just relax and trust Him through them all. So also can you.

Nothing gets made instantly, everything goes through its own journey, your dream or call may not even be like mine, it may be rising up in your career to prominence or growing a business or starting something new, whatever it is, go through your process, do not take shortcuts because they can be very costly.

CHAPTER 6

DEAL WITH THE FOXES

WE are imperfect people in an imperfect world and everyone has an area that they must keep growing in, progressively mastering and conquering so that, the greatness in them can truly manifest in a wholesome way that can give God glory and bless humanity.

Moses was a man called and chosen by God to carry out the assignment of leading over four million Jews from slavery into the Promised Land. He was also a man given to quick and short temper and this came to light whenever he was provoked. The whole purpose of leading those people out of slavery was to get them into the Promised Land but it never came to pass for him.

Agreed, he did not lead an easy crowd, they got on his last nerve and pushed his button many times but unfortunately, his temper got the best of him. He reacted in anger towards the people and his reaction in a particular situation turned out to be a disobedience to God's instruction that cost him the Promised Land. *(Numbers 20:12).*

When you read a story like this, it is very easy to feel empathy towards Moses and put the blame on the people but the lesson I believe we can all learn here is that, people and circumstances may hurl stones at us many times, our reaction is our responsibility. If Moses had gained mastery over his anger issues, he would not have been affected by the Jews to the point of missing the Promised Land.

His calling took him so far, God did many miracles through him that generations after, we are still talking about them but it was this aspect of his life that disqualified him from witnessing the fullness of God's promises.

How can we finish strong if we do not gain mastery over the things that easily cut us short and make us miss the mark? It has often been said that, someone can preach an anointed message and still live an immoral life. Why is this so? The gifts and calling of God are without repentance, the fact that God is patient with us and suffers long for us does not mean we should take His grace and mercy for granted.

If we must fulfill His purpose in our lives we must deal with the little foxes that spoil the vine.

How are the mighty fallen! In our world today, many leaders have been brought down from grace to disgrace because they were caught in one questionable act or another.

Not because they were unable to function in their gift, talent or calling but because a character flaw overtook them and it became exposed.

When I hear of stories like this, it makes me humble and sober to pay close attention to me and any area I need God to help me win battles over. No one is immune to this so we must not become judgmental of others, rather pray for them and soberly pay attention to our own "tendencies".

I must constantly check myself and know that, as a spirit being in this human flesh, I must never rely on me or be puffed up as if I am above temptations. I am daily covered and sustained by the grace of God because I tap into it. I know for me that, I must always plug into my Source for strength because He is the only One that will never fail.

The devil knows how to set the bait and he is too clever to set it in a way that one can really recognize. Rather, he will use something that is familiar, a weak spot you've neglected that has become a part and parcel of you. I don't think he will tempt you to get angry to the point of sinning if you don't have serious anger issues because he knows that, you will easily recognize it and because it is not your weak spot, you can easily defeat that temptation.

But he will use something that can respond to the remote control he has against you. If we are honest and sincere with ourselves, we know where our buttons can be pushed, we know our weak spots.

One major intention of the enemy is not just to bring us down and embarrass us in front of others, those are extras that come along with his plan. I truly believe that, his major plan is to terminate the purpose of God for our lives. The devil kills, steals and destroys **(John 10:10)** says and he will use everything possible to do this and one area he does that, is through using our weaknesses to get us. I call them foxes, we must deal with them with God's help. The power to do that is already in us, we just have to activate and walk in it.

Let's examine some steps through which we can easily deal with this;

1.   RECOGNIZE THE FOXES IN YOUR LIFE

Be ruthlessly sincere with yourself and recognize what they are. Is it lust, pride, anger, selfish ambition, strong headedness, compulsive lying, fear, jealousy, envy, wrath, toying with sin, abusing the grace of God, idolatry or lukewarmness? The list goes on and on. You know you and God knows you better. Any of these things in our lives we are able to overcome by His word and the help of His Holy Spirit.

2. CRY OUT TO GOD.

It is comforting to know that, God hears us when we call, He knows what we are going to say before we call on Him. He knows all our frailties and weaknesses and He knows how best to help us. The scriptures say, ***"We do not have a High Priest who cannot sympathize with our weaknesses, but was in all points tempted as we are, yet without sin."*** *(Hebrews 4:15)* When we cry out to Him to help us, He is ever ready to act. I remember having to cry out to God in many cases but particularly when I dealt with a lot of anger issues and God in His mercies began to help me every step of the way. How? Let's see the next point.

3. POWER IN THE WORD.

If only people would recognize how much power lies in the word of God, we would not want to separate ourselves from it. It is a life giving source. Find out what the scriptures say about whatever you are dealing with and apply it into your life constantly. Wow! That sounds simple. The truth is that, the ways of God are not complicated at all, we are the ones that complicate them.

Personally, after having cried out to God, I went into the word of God and got scriptures that deal with anger. The word became alive in me and showed me exactly where I was and where I could be headed if I did not

deal with it. For example; the Bible says in Ecclesiastes
7:9; *"Do not hasten in your spirit to be angry, for*
anger lies in the bosom of fools" I am not a fool, I said
to myself but then my eyes became open to the fact that,
as long as I allowed anger to dwell in my bosom, I was
one. Even that is still hard to swallow up till now but it
is the truth. This was how I practically began to separate
myself from this flaw and allow the word of God to help
me till its grip on me broke.

4. **WATCH OUT**

The fact that you deal with a weakness does not mean
you will not be tempted in that area again. How would
you know you have mastered it if you don't pass the tests
that are thrown your way? Till this day, anger tries to
show up but God has so much helped me and His grace
has given me the ability to gain mastery over it. It's all by
allowing the word of God to take roots in our hearts and
play itself out in our lives daily. Many times, I encounter
things that just want to make me "lose it" and act the old
way but because I am intentionally working on myself in
this area, by God's grace, I win.

5. **TALK ABOUT IT**

I hope it makes sense to you as the reader of this book
that, when you actually talk about what you are over-
coming, you strip that weakness of its power over you
and you hold yourself accountable publicly. This is what
I have just done in the previous point about myself.
Talk about it, separate yourself from it and declare your
victory over it.

6. REMAIN IN THE WORD

Living your life on the concept of victory is an ongoing process. It is not something you do once and keep on the shelf. You must stay in the word of God continually. The more you stay in it, the more victorious you become.

7. DO NOT GIVE ROOM TO THE FLESH

Like I said, the temptation will come to tempt you to fall into that old ways or give in to the weaknesses but do not cooperate with it neither give it any room. If you are a person who is given to anger, don't provoke others and when you are provoked, take the high road, walk away, keep silent, don't get into an argument because it only stirs up strife.

8. HAVE AN ACCOUNTABILITY PARTNER

I recommend being accountable to others because there are some weaknesses that, you will need the help of others to keep you in check. Open up to people you respect and trust, that you know really love you and you can take advice from them even if it hurts. Let them in to help you. My biological mom, my spiritual parents and my husband have been my sounding board for years and God has used them tremendously to help me in a lot of ways. I have learned not to be defensive when flaws are pointed out knowing fully well that, my identity is not wrapped up in the flaws. God loves and accepts me regardless of them but He also loves me enough to want me to live a victorious life, fulfilling purpose without these flaws destroying me.

This is the reason why, everyone must have someone in their lives that they are willing to receive from no matter how difficult the truth may sound. If you surround yourself with people who only agree with you, there is a problem because you can only grow so far in life with that. "YES" people will not tell you the truth, either they are too afraid to or because they do not want your feelings hurt. Either way, it is not healthy to surround yourself only with people who agree with you all the time.

Dealing with the foxes in your life is your personal responsibility and the power to deal with it dwells in you, don't feed the foxes, don't nurture them because they are tools in the hand of the enemy to terminate the purpose of God in one's life so give those foxes no room!

CHAPTER 7

ACCEPT YOURSELF FIRST- BECOME A BETTER ORIGINAL YOU

GOD is a God of varieties. He has not created everyone the same way, we have different races, different languages, different skin colors, different personalities and all these things are what make the world exciting. Imagine if the whole world were to be just one race and one color? What a boring world that would be!

It also happens that, you don't get to choose what race you would come from or who your birth parents would be. These are two major things that are completely out of your control and that is the reason why, we must accept ourselves as God has created us, love ourselves because only then , can we learn to love others. Embrace your uniqueness and those things that make you you because they are all part of God's divine design.

Many times, we try to be like other people to the point where we lose our own originality. It is okay, to emulate good qualities from other people but even where that is concerned, when delivering it, your personality and who you are, will and should shine through. It is through your true self that, you can truly operate, bless people and be fulfilled in life.

How can the giant within you shine forth when you don't even notice it because you are busy looking at what someone else is and wishing you were them? Life might have treated you unfairly but God can use every experience to work for your good. *(Romans 8:28)*

There are times when things we cannot control or understand happen but we know that, there is a God who understands the end from the beginning, He sees the full picture and He is able to make all things turn out rightly in accordance with His will and purpose for us.

There may be things that we may have to fine tune and work on in our lives to make us become better people and you will find out that, in that, your true self will still be preserved. I remember looking at my husband and wishing that, I was as cool and calm as he is, I even tried talking quietly like he would, acting like I was a very quiet person. People who knew me would ask if everything was okay with me and when I said yes, they would ask why I was talking and acting weirdly because I was not myself. I had no answer! I was miserable, totally miserable, why? Because I was not wired that way for crying out loud! Needless to say that it lasted only for a very short time. That was not how God formed me. Any attempt to be what we are not will end up making us miserable.

However, I also discovered that, the reason why I wanted to be something I was not, was because I did not like some things about myself and I felt that, the best way to change that was to be someone else and that did not go well. What I discovered I was supposed to do and ended up doing that made me fall totally in love with myself, was bringing those things I did not like before God, asking for His grace to change and passing several tests that came my way. I became a better person, a better original me.

There are many changes that took place in my life and that continue to take place as I move on in life but I will share one that,

I continue to work on with you. I was a highly sensitive person in the sense that, I wore my emotions on my sleeves and reacted to so many things if not everything. I could read into a body language, an unpleasant tone in someone's voice, an act of rudeness and other things in that sense. The worst part of it was that, instead of me to ignore, walk away or act differently, no! I always welcomed the fight, reacted, confronted and gave my piece of mind.

I heard this from my spiritual mother that, "maturity is the ability to delay gratification." I sure did not delay any gratification during that time, I responded in ways that ended up making me sad on the inside and making people around me feel very uncomfortable. I was trapped in this state for such a long time because I always told myself that, this was the way God made me and it was either people accepted it or left me alone.

That statement in itself was an excuse not to become better and change my ways. When I hear people say that now, I remember how far God has brought me and I know that, anyone can change if they are willing to.

When I married my husband, I carried this attitude into marriage. He on the other hand is what you call, cool, calm and collected, he is just the same, does not get ruffled by anything, he is just as calm and peaceful as you can imagine, almost all the time. This first of all irritated me that, someone would not just have a moment to react and raise their voice, then when I moved from being irritated and I tried to be like him as I said earlier and I was miserable.

Ultimately, I went into the word of God and began to study scriptures that talk about what I was dealing with. I found the book of Proverbs and Ecclesiastes to be very useful and at the same time very chastening. It was not funny. Many scriptures in there dealt positive but painful blows on me. The more I went into the word and allowed it to shape me, the more a better me began to emerge. A happier me, a more friendly me, a more temperate me, a passionately gentle me, many people that know me now may find it hard to believe I used to be like that but people that used to know me well in times past will readily testify to how much I have changed.

I did not need to be someone else but I needed to first of all accept myself and recognize that there was room for growth. In order to be that person whose aroma the world wants to be around, a lot of dying to self, crucifixion of the flesh must be done. I love me now, I may not be where I want to be but I am definitely not where I used to be.

A lot of people cannot accept themselves and want to be like someone else in one area or the other. If you fall into this category, you may want to dig deep within and ask yourself some questions. It may be that, you just need to become a better you that you yourself can fall in love with and you will find it very thrilling accepting yourself.

Shedding some more light on this topic of accepting yourself, it can be as serious as not liking your skin color, your race or your background wishing everything was something else.

If you don't accept the things you cannot change, you will pass through life resenting everything including yourself and fail miserably at being happy.

I can't change my race or the color of my skin, I did not ask to be born an African or Black, I did not choose the family I was born into or the background I grew up in, these are some of the things out of my control and in your case too, they are out of your control so to not accept myself in these areas is to be saying that God made a mistake and God never makes mistakes.

Everything has been divinely designed, He knew before He

formed me that, I would be a black woman, born in Nigeria, West Africa and I bless Him for that because I have been uniquely made. I love my skin color, I don't want to be lighter or darker, I just love it the way it has been given to me. I love my home country and I have been privileged to have many great memories about my country. With me being born and raised there for over three decades before I came to America also came my accent. I love it, it has been a conversation starter for me many times. People would often say ' I notice an accent, where are you from? There goes the introduction of my country again. I am comfortable in my own skin by the grace and favor of God and because of this, it draws people to me as well.

One thing I found difficult to accept growing up was being super skinny because I was called names and I allowed those names to define me. This went on till I was about nineteen years of age. I remember being home from a prolonged college break for about six months and I had one mission, just one mission, which was to eat as much as possible and gain as much weight as possible before school would reopen. I ate and ate and maybe gained something but nothing substantial for anyone to even say, "Oh wow! You sure did add some weight during the break".

That did it for me. Again I began to do a soul search, I talk to God a lot, that is one major way I have been able to keep my sanity. I realized for the first time after this eating binge that, I was not formed to be fat, I took after my dad who is very slim, his genes run in my body so I either accept it or live a life of misery. I began to accept myself, wear clothes my real size instead of hiding under big clothes pretending to be bigger than I really was. I began to enjoy my stature and I saw that, it was not that bad, it was not even bad at all. I am a slim girl and that's it.

I made up my mind to enjoy myself and carry myself with a

sense of dignity. I dare to say that, the name calling stopped and to my shock! People began to commend my stature with loads of people asking if I was a model or advising that, I became one, this still happens up to this day. What changed? Me! I changed, I accepted myself and people began to accept me the way I am. My goal is to be fit and healthy, thanks to motherhood, I have gained a few pounds and I love it but my goal now is to stay healthy and fit and not try to be what I am not.

If you don't love yourself, you will find it hard to love others. If you don't accept yourself, you cannot love yourself. There may be things you want to visit and change with God's help and other resources out there but ultimately, all these should take you to a place where you can look at yourself in the mirror and be completely full of gratitude to God for making you so uniquely wonderful!

Loving and accepting yourself starts from within and when you have dealt with what is on the inside, the outside will line up.

CHAPTER 8

YOU DESERVE GOD'S BEST

SOMETIMES in our lives, we think that, if we can just get by in this life it is okay. If I can just have a roof over my head and food on my table, that's all, I don't need anything else. But the truth is that, God wants us to live abundantly well, not only materially speaking but in every aspect of life. The Bible says, that,.... *"God takes pleasure in the prosperity of His people." (Psalm 35:27b)* Prosperity in that sense is an all encompassing word.

You may ask, what about all the bad things that happen and sometimes drain the life out of people? Well, it's true they happen but it is not God throwing them at us, the Holy Scriptures say that, satan has come to kill, steal and destroy but Christ has come to give us abundant life. **(John 10:10)** Here in this life, we have to stand our ground against the forces of darkness to enjoy the abundant life that God has given us.

He loved us so much that, He gave us His very best, He gave us His only begotten Son and the Bible says that, if He did not withhold Him from us, He will freely give us all things. *(Romans 8:32)* What a joy! You and I deserve His best not because we earned it because we can never earn it but because it has been freely given to us by God.

Whatever it is, that may be warring against your spirit, soul and body, trying to keep you in a box, trying to paint a picture of a life that God has not ordained for you, is a lie and you must rise up in the confidence of knowing that, God is on your side and He wants His best for you and you must create room to receive it.

Yes, heaven is a place of joy, streets of gold and eternal life with Christ but in this present life, we can live out God's promises, we can live life to the fullest with God on our side every step of the way. Yes! We will work hard, we will apply effort diligently no matter what we do but His best is for us here now while we are living.

What if you don't know that, God wants to prosper you or what if you know but you don't really believe it deep within you, the result is that, you will just get by based on your level of knowledge and belief. He cannot manifest Himself to you beyond your level of knowledge of Him. You can wallow in lack and poverty and be a Christian if you do not know that, it gives God great joy to see you prosperous and live a fulfilled life.

Whether you know Him or not, He loved you enough to send His Son, His only Son. The Scriptures say that, *"For God so loved the world that He gave His only begotten Son so that, whosoever believes in Him would not perish but have everlasting life."* *(John 3:16)* He has given everyone a free invitation to belong and all you have to do is accept it and His best would be yours.

It would be a waste to live less than God's intended best for us. We can excel in every area of our lives when we walk closely with Him. If you don't know Him, you may want to ask that, is it only people that know Him that will excel? No, is the answer, there are many people who do not know God who are doing extremely well because they are applying certain laws and principles. But for those who know Him, there are lots of extra perks that are available to them that are not available to others.

For example, prosperity of the soul is not anything money or influence can buy, it comes as a result of knowing God. When your soul prospers, your mind is at rest no matter what, it does not matter the situation you may be in, you know you are not alone, even when you feel alone, you are still not alone because God is with you. Also for those who do not know Him, everything ends here on earth, the wealth, the glamour, the achievements all end here on earth for them. For those who know Him, earth is a temporary place, His blessings of eternal life await them when this life is over.

We have the privilege of knowing that all His great and precious promises in His word are ours and we can stand on those words and move forward in faith to experience His best in this life and in the life to come.

The mentality that, one should just exist by struggling to survive is one that, I don't believe God derives any joy from. Life is in phases as we all know but there must be a progression as we journey through it. Everything we would ever need has already been provided for, we must first of all free our minds to accept that God wants His best for us, then we must accept and embrace it before we can actually experience it.

What if you deposited a million dollars in a bank account for your young adult child and he is living broke, even though he knows the money has been deposited in his name but yet he does not make the effort to get up, drive to the bank and claim owner-ship of the money. Instead, he is sitting in lack and wallowing in self-pity, complaining about how things are really tough for him. If he remains in that, state, he will continue to suffer but all he needs to do is to get up and to claim what belongs to him and use it wisely to generate more.

For those who claim to know God as their father and still

live in a state that is less than God's best, today, I challenge you
to arise, get into the word of God and find out all His promises
regarding your situation, declare them, meditate on them, take
steps of faith towards any instructions that the Lord may drop in
your heart. Yes, fear may grip you but do it afraid anyway and you
will experience many breakthroughs.

He says in His word that, He wishes that,.... **"you may
prosper in ALL things and be in health, just as your soul
prospers. (3John1:2)."** So if this is God's will for us, we should
be prosperous if we truly know what is ours. God's best for me is
to live in divine health and there had been many times, when sick-
nesses attacked my body but because I am fully aware of God's
mind regarding my health, I have had to fight to stay my ground
spiritually, declaring His promises over the situations while maintaining a healthy lifestyle physically.

As I shared in one of the chapters about how fearful I used
to be but how by the grace of God, I am free from fear now and
even when it tries to creep in again, I know just how to confront
it- by the word of God. That was how I overcame that tormenting
trial in my life that had me bound for a long time, His word was
my weapon day and night. I cannot say how long it took for me to
be totally free but I know that, I was committed and a time came
when the word took over and drowned the voice of fear in my
mind.

It was not God's best for me to live in fear, living in that kind
of torment was living below God's best for my life. There was
a work I needed to do to renew my mind, freedom was already
available to me but I needed to step up and claim it over and over
again. This is where a lot of people fall short, when it comes to
the work part. It would have been easy if someone could have
just laid their hands on me and the fear vanished, no! I had to

take ownership of the promise of God and reject fear with all my might. While it is okay for people to lay hands on you and pray for you, you still have a responsibility to stand your ground against anything the enemy may be sending your way and walk in victory.

I hope that, if you do not know Jesus as your Lord and Savior, this chapter would have shown you how there are many priceless promises in the word, such that money cannot buy, available to those who have surrendered to Him and you will be able to make an intelligent decision of inviting Him into your heart.

God's best is for us and we must agree with that truth and allow Him to show His glory in and through us.

CHAPTER 9

KEEP YOUR EYES ON THE FINISH LINE

I F you are in a race of any sort in life, you must first see your-self crossing the finish line because that is the major way you will get there. There may be many obstacles along the way but if you run your race with a focused determination of finishing it, you will get there.

Obstacles sometimes may pose as stumbling blocks in our lives, it is called life, and it is full of ups and downs. When we lean on the grace of God, He helps us to overcome the obstacles and they become stepping stones to greater heights. It does not matter what the race that is set before you is, the grace of God is sufficient for you to run it to the end and finish strong if you tap into that grace.

A runner in a race may get tired along the way, it is a natural thing because he is exerting a lot of energy, he may even slow down a bit to catch his breath or have a drink of water, sometimes, he may trip and fall but he gets back up again, he keeps going, he does not quit because he has set his mind to cross the finish line. If he gets weary and gives up along the way, if when he falls, he does not get back up, reaching that finish line is no longer in view, it is lost.

Finish line may mean different things to different people. To someone who is working on shedding off some weight, going to the gym and exercising, eating right and living a healthy lifestyle that support their goal become their race. Their body may become sore, the diet may feel like a punishment compared to what they were used to but because they are focused on crossing the finish line and shedding off that unwanted weight, they must persevere and keep going no matter how hard it gets because when the results are in and the weight is off, the sacrifice will be well worth it.

If you are a business person, who desires to reach a certain career level, doing all it takes to get there becomes your race. Along the way, there may be disappointments that will be experienced, rejections, several cancelled appointments, unreached goals at set times but if you will keep going and not give up, if you will get back up every time you fall and stay in the game, sticking to your goals without letting go, not wavering in the face of obstacles, doing all the activities that are necessary, you will get there. You will reach your goals, you will get to that career level that you so desire. When you cross that finish line, you will experience victory and a sense of fulfillment.

Come to think of it, if you study the lives of very successful people in history, they went through a lot of challenges but what made them become part of history is that, they never gave up. Many of them faced insurmountable obstacles but they refused to give up. Who is someone that history remembers as a successful person that you know of, go and study that person's life, you will find out quickly that, somewhere along the way, they faced many obstacles but they just refused to give up.

To us Christians running the race of life, we must keep our eyes on the Author and Finisher of our faith- Jesus Christ. The Bible says that, *"....who for the joy that was set before Him, endured the cross, despising the shame"... (Hebrews 12:2 (NKJV))*

He became the ultimate example for us that, in this world, there may be many ups and downs, many trials and tribulations but if we will keep our eyes on Him, we will finish strong, we will reign with Him. Our destination as Christians is Christlikeness, that is; to be like Christ. I believe everyday as we walk with Him in Spirit and in Truth, we are changed into His likeness. It should be that, when an unbeliever comes in contact with a Christian that is walking with Jesus, they should experience the very essence of Christ. Howbeit, we cannot get there in a day so as we die to self daily, crucifying the flesh and living a life in the Spirit, we will cross the finish line and the world will see Him in us.

As I mentioned earlier on in this chapter, it is important to see yourself crossing the finish line in your mind before you even start the race. You may visualize where you will be by the time the race is over. In this process, there is also the realistic anticipation of trials and challenges that may come up along the way but you must make up your mind before you even start that, no matter what comes along the way, you will finish your race and you will cross the finish line.

The best example is the Lord Jesus Christ, who came to this earth for the singular purpose of redeeming the world and reconciling people back to God. He knew beforehand that, He would sacrifice His life in a most gruesome way; He saw the death on the cross before He was ever hung on it but He despised it. He went through it, He finished His race, He crossed His finish line and as a result of this, everyone who comes to believe in Him is reconciled with God and given the right as a child of God. What if He had quit along the way, He had the power to say no to the cross so

what if, when the time came, He turned His back on the plan of
God, there would have been no redemption story.

This tells me that, when you choose to finish your race and
cross the finish line, God will be glorified, purpose will be fulfilled,
you will be blessed and many great things will happen. Many things
that are beyond even you as a person will happen.

There are some things to consider when you think of crossing
the finish line, let's examine them.

1. WHO IS IN YOUR POWER CIRCLE?

It is important to know that, you were not made to do
life alone. It is crucial that, you surround yourself with
people who place a value on you, constructively help you
and relentlessly support you in your journey.

When Jesus was in the garden of Gethsemane and He
was about to be arrested and handed over for crucifixion, He agonized so much that, the sweat on his brow
was bloody but the Bible records that, angels came and
strengthened Him, talk about power circle, He rose
from that garden and faced all the sorrows before Him
triumphantly.

When you have a power circle, they can encourage you
when life gets tough and the race becomes rough, they
can hold your hand and keep you from falling, they can
cheer you on when you get tired and weary, they can
speak life into you when it feels like you can't go on
again. They see the vision with you, they understand the
purpose of God for your life and they are committed to
helping you cross that finish line.

You may want to ask yourself, who are the people in my power circle? Recognize them and keep them close. You may also be a power partner for someone else as well, if this is the case, know that, you hold an important role in that person's life, value it and give everything within your power to help them cross their finish line. It is always a joy and a blessing to be part of someone else's success.

2. AVOID DISTRACTIONS

It is natural for distractions to come up along the way to take your eyes off the finish line. For instance, if a runner is running on a track field, he can get distracted by many things, people's applauses, fellow runners, fatigue and breathlessness etc. It is the same in life, there will be both good and bad distractions that will arise but you must determine not to get carried away by them. Good distractions may come in form of recognition and achievements along the way. It is possible to get sucked into the euphoria of this and lose focus of the finish line. While it is okay to acknowledge recognition, do it and move on immediately, don't dwell on it, don't let it derail you from your purpose.

Bad distraction can also come in form of failures, negative criticism, the feeling of being left behind and so on, though these bring hurts along with them, huge disappointments and sometimes heartbreaks but you must choose not to allow them to have power over you.

It is said that, the power people have over you is the power you give to them. I believe it is not only people but also situations and circumstances as well. A situation can only control you for as long as you allow it to, the moment you stand your ground and allow change to take positive effect, you take your power back. Someone once said that, "if the devil cannot keep your goods, he cannot steal your joy". Take charge and guard your heart securely.

3. KEEP THE PICTURE ALIVE

It is important to always have a mental picture of what the finish line will look like. Keep it alive, keep it fresh every time because when the going gets tough, this picture will remind you of the reason why you are in the race in the first place.

There is a true story of one man and his friend who went fishing, their boat capsized and they fell into the deep sea, one drowned and died, while the other man was rescued after a few days. He was found hanging unto the boat, tired, hungry and suffering from hypothermia. After he was rescued and he became well enough, he spoke about holding the picture of hugging his mom in his mind and that helped him to fight through the life threatening ordeal he went through, he held on to it till he was rescued and got to hug his mom. What is your finish line? Pause. Think about it. What is the end result of your race? What will it be like, when you finally reach that goal? Keep that picture alive within you.

It has often been said that, whatever you focus on will grow bigger. What if you focus on the picture of the end result of your goal? Whatever obstacles you may face along the way will not matter, they will not derail you from forging ahead, with focused determination, you will get to the finish line, the picture will become a reality, you will experience that end result.

For the joy that was set before Jesus Christ, He despised the shame of the cross. I encourage you to keep your eyes on the finish line. Let your gaze be fixed on it because there and there only can you reap the reward of a well-run race.

Sometimes, living life as a follower of Christ can be challenging in this present world but when I think of the fact that, this is not where the journey ends, there is a heaven awaiting all those who have given their lives to Him, those who are honoring Him with their existence. I am greatly encouraged to continue in this race no matter what trials and tribulations may come my way because He has already called me an overcomer, the same goes for you if you have accepted Him as your Lord and personal Savior.

Your finish line may be finishing a particular project to the end and in the course of carrying it out, you encounter a lot of obstacles, setbacks and disappointments, I encourage you today to hold on tight and keep your focus intact. Keep the end result in view constantly and keep on going until you get there. Don't quit along the way, just stay the course, your finish line will come to pass.

CHAPTER 10

FAITH EMPOWERS, FEAR PARALYZES

THE place of faith is the place of power! It is the place where you look up and soar like an eagle. It is the place of risk taking with total abandonment to God's mercy, grace and will. It is the place where you will be sorely tested but where you must trust in God's absolute power and authority.

The place of fear on the other hand is the place of paralysis. It is the place where dreams become stuck in a rut and the dreamer is unable to move forward towards his/her goal. It is a place where as a result of fear, a lot of excuses emerge and dreams fade away.

Fear will stop you in your tracks but faith will catapult you to victory! Work from the place of faith and go for the gold. Many people have described fear as a "False Evidence Appearing Real" that means, fear has no basis. It is amazing to see how imprisoning fear can be even though it has no substance. It can paralyze a person, demobilize them from living their best life. As negative as fear is, it is a force that can stop many from fulfilling their God given purpose.

Many of us don't like to face our fears so we would rather allow it to continue to dominate us instead of confronting it. The day a person decides they've had enough and would not live their life in bondage to fear anymore is the day they receive their freedom to live life to the fullest, to fulfill their God-given purpose. A lot of people don't admit that they are walking in fear, on the surface many reasons are given why they can't do this or that but when truthfully examined, the underlying factor can be fear sometimes.

I heard the story of a man who travelled far away from home to go and study a group of people who lived in the wild jungle. They looked and acted wild and for some time after he got there, he could do nothing because he was afraid that he might be hurt or even get killed. A day came when he got tired of being afraid and began to talk to himself and confront his worst fears, he faced his ultimate fear which was the possibility that, this group of people might kill him and he decided to act despite that fear. He extended a hand of fellowship to them and gradually, they began to warm up to him until they totally accepted him among them. He was able to learn about them and fulfill the purpose he went there for.

When his colleagues heard about his breakthrough of having favor with these people, they were shocked because no one had had the success of going to this place and to study them. When the man was asked how he did it, he simply replied by saying that, he confronted his worst fear and it no longer had any power over him.

I am encouraged by the scriptures always because that is where I find my own strength to tackle any challenge I may be facing. This is the source I tap into to confront fears every time.

In 2006, I was approached by a friend to start a business and for two years, I gave many excuses why I could not do it. I said, I would pray about it until God told me to start it, I used anything and everything to say no to it. Really, it was the fear of the unknown that held me captive, fear of failure, fear of rejection etc. It was not until I confronted these fears in prayer and decided to step out of the boat did I experience victory. I remember feeling afraid and still going forward anyway, quoting scriptures like, *"I can do all things through Christ who strengthens me."* *(Philippians 4:13)* Declaring scriptures like this and allowing them to take roots within my heart while corresponding it with the activities required in the business helped me overcome.

It was so humbling and at the same time amazing to see how I rose to the leadership position in the business. This was me, who stayed in a corner, allowing fear to rule me until I had had enough. The only regret I had in this particular situation was the fact that, I gave fear permission to have a hold on me for two years and I wasted that time giving excuses that had no basis.

I also see fear as a bait of the enemy of our soul to keep us from fulfilling God's purpose for our lives. Our mind can play many games on us, as I said earlier; it has been said that, the mind is the battlefield and the battle is either won or lost in our mind. If we allow it, fear will turn our mind into a playground. It is comforting to know that, we were not just thrown into this earth without any help. As many as would take advantage of it, God has made a way out through His word. It is not only enough to know God, it is important to also know the principles by which He operates and when these are embraced, amazing victories will happen. He has not promised a trial free life but He has assured us that, He would be with us every step of the way.

I have seen the power of God at work in many areas of my life since I became a Believer. For a long time, I struggled with fear and anxiety, even after I became a born again Believer, I ignorantly suffered from their effects. I was afraid of many things, situations and people. I was miserable and lacked peace and joy most times. It reflected in my moods and the way I related with people. It did not only affect me but it affected the people in my life. Nothing good ever comes from tormenting fear.

Now I can look back and trace this and see how much the
enemy took advantage of my ignorance. I wish I could say I overcame this situation shortly after I became a Believer but no! I did
not, I was already an adult, a wife, a mom and a Christian who was
actively serving God yet being defeated at the same time because I
did not claim what was rightfully mine in God.

It was not that, the Word of God did not work in my life, it
was simply that, I did not walk in the power and authority that
had been given to me in this particular area of my life. I had been
schooled in the word because I had the privilege of learning from
excellent Teachers of the word but had I applied it in this particular situation? The answer is no because had I applied it rightly, I
would have experienced victory.

It was not until, I saw how the situation affected the people
closest to me that I began to see how I was not only allowing
myself to be robbed but my loved ones were directly or indirectly
being robbed too.

There was a period in my life that, I could not drive on the
highways because of fear and bless his heart, Emmanuel, my
husband was taking me everywhere that involved highways and
as if that was not enough, we would have to take my kids along
because they could not be left home alone.

One particular four hour trip did it for me, as usual, we had
made the trip and since it was my business trip, my husband and
kids were stuck in the hotel while I used the car to attend my business appointments within that city. I would go and pick them in
between my appointments to go to the restaurant to eat and drop
them back at the hotel then run to my remaining appointments.
It was stressful for me and not fun for the ones stuck at the hotel
while I used the car.

I remember talking to my husband on our way back on this

trip and telling him that I had to face this fear and drive myself next time. He was very kind to go on the next four-hour trip with me but he allowed me to drive all the way to and fro. I felt elated, I could now drive on the highway!

The real test came when I had to go on this trip all by myself, no Emmanuel to go with me, no kids to chat with on the way, it was just me and my invisible God. Fearful whisperings of the enemy rang loud in my head, the moment of truth presented itself, I was already on the road and could not turn back. It was like being on the battlefield. The word of God that, I had known for decades before came alive within me, I began to confront the fear that plagued me with the word of God in **2Timothy 1:7** that says; *"For God has not given us a spirit of fear but of power and of love and of a sound mind"*. I confessed it loudly, I took authority over that spirit of fear and shut down its voice until it disappeared.

Was I afraid? Absolutely yes! But I also knew that, it was either I allowed myself to be continually tormented by this spirit or stand in the place of power and live in victory. There were moments of anxiety and fear here and there but I drove all the way! I attended all my appointments with ease and focus. I remember meeting some of my business partners who knew about the fact that I dealt with fear and could not drive on the highway unless my husband took me. When they found out that I drove myself, to them, it was unbelievable, "did you come alone?" they asked. I said, "oh no! God the Father, the Son and the Holy Spirit were all with me and they helped me to drive."

The truth of the matter was that, I meant that statement literally because I invoked the presence of God on that trip and I could feel it all around me in the car. There were times on the highway when I would overtake a semi- truck and wondered how I

did it, there was a force at work within me, a force that was greater
than fear and anxiety, it was the power of God.

On my way back home it was easier and when that fear began
to rumble again, I knew exactly what to do. This was how I overcame this and it spread to other areas of my life where I was afraid.
I began to exercise the authority of God's word in those areas of
my life and little by little, I began to experience victory. Does fear
still come? Yes, it does but I also know that, I will never be a victim
to it anymore because I now live from the place of power that is
within me and I exercise it fully.

Now, to someone else, my story may not be a big deal or even
be a dramatic one that catches much attention but it was my reality,
I lived in that prison even though Christ had set me free. All the
while, when I was in that bondage, God was God, the word was
true as always but I was not living in the realization of the power
and authority I had been given. No one could do that for me, I
had to step up and take responsibility as a true child of God, then,
only then did victory happen in my life. Now I am living from the
place of power.

Even as I write this particular chapter, I think of how many
people live in bondage yet they have power given to them by God
to live above those circumstances. While miracles do occur, some
things are not automatic, you have to work at it, you have to stand
up and exercise your God-given authority. I have heard Believers
beg God for what He has already given them. Imagine me asking
and begging God to take away the spirit of fear that plagued me.....
that would be out of place somehow. I did not need to beg Him,
I just needed to accept what He had already done and walk in the
revelation of that knowledge. This is what I call living from the
place of power and it can be exercised in every area of our lives.

There are ways by which we can allow ourselves to walk in faith rather than submit to fear.

1. **CONFRONT YOUR FEARS**

    One major thing I have found out is that, when you confront the things you are afraid of and analyze the worst case scenario, you strip fear of its power of holding you captive. In the case of the business I talked about earlier, I had to confront my fears before I could move ahead. My friend asked me, "what is the worst thing that could happen to you if you said yes to this business" suffice to say, I answered and spoke my fears out loud...."I might not make it, I might lose money, people might not buy from me and so on and so forth". She then asked me, "What is the best thing that could happen"? I answered that, "I could make it, be successful, have impact on others and stuff". She said; "how would you know which one would happen if you never tried?" Right there, I had no more excuses. It was true that, I would never know if I never tried.

    Many people are held back because of fear because they have not confronted their fears, if you are in that category in any area of your life, I encourage you to no longer give fear any room to flex its muscles. One of the ways you can strip it of that privilege is by confronting it. Do what you are afraid of.

2. **CHOOSE NOT TO BE AFRAID.**

    Being afraid is a choice and one of the gifts God has given us is the power of choice. You can simply choose not to be afraid. I know it sounds easy but it is easy. Choose to rise above your fears. You may feel afraid but you don't have to yield to it. Talk to yourself and say the exact opposite of what fear wants you to say however it may apply to you. For example; when I was overcoming the fear of going into business, I would declare that, my future was bright and I would be a successful business woman. I spoke back to the fear of the unknown. I declared scriptures that talk about how to overcome fears. Don't deal with fear in your thoughts, speak back to it. Declare the word of God to counter fear. Search the scriptures and find out what the word says and confront fear with the truth of God's word.

3.   FEED YOUR MIND WITH POSITIVITY

The mind is a powerful tool, what you put into it is what you get out of it. The Bible says that, " **A good man out of the good treasure of his heart brings forth good; and an evil man out of the evil treasure of his heart brings forth evil. For out of the abundance of the heart, his mouth speaks."** (Luke 6:45).

What do you feed your mind with? Many people watch things that sow the seeds of fear into their hearts. They listen to news that steal their faith, they surround themselves with people that constantly tear them down and rob them of their confidence in God. If you find yourself in any of these situations, you want to make a 360 degree turn around and begin to change the course of fear in your life. The Bible says that; *"faith comes by hearing and hearing by the word of God".* *(Romans*

10:17) The word of God brings hope to the hopeless and health for the soul. Fear also comes by hearing
the negative words of the enemy so make sure you are
hearing what will feed your faith and starve your fear.

4. **ACT**

There is no more powerful way to counter fear than
action. After making a decision to not be afraid,
declaring affirmative words to build your faith, the next
most important thing is to act. Rather than wishing and
hoping that somehow, someway, fear would go away and
things would change, just step out boldly in faith and act.

You will find out at first that, you may almost want to
jump out of your body for acting but if you will stick it
out and act, you will overcome it and gradually, things
will get easier until fear is no more and in many cases,
once you confront it and act, you don't see fear again
and if by any chance, fear comes again knocking on your
door, you know exactly how to deal with it.

5. **BE COMMITTED**

It is possible to lose the grounds you've already gained if
you are not committed in consistently maintaining your
stance. You must make up your mind that, no matter
what shows up, you will forge ahead. It is so much like
life for new challenges to show up that test our faith and
confidence every now and then. This is the reason why
your feet must be firmly established. Like I said earlier,
I have found a firm foundation in staying rooted in the
Holy Scriptures and these help me from time to time as

I journey through life. Applying them into my life practically has brought tremendous results that cannot be adequately expressed in words.

6. DO NOT BE AFRAID OF FAILURE

What if you tried and you failed? So what? At least you tried. You did better than those who never made an effort to try. The fact that you failed does not make you a failure, you just discovered another way not to do things. When you try the next time, you know what to do and what to avoid. This was Thomas Edison's attitude towards the making of electric lightbulb, What if he was afraid that making of electric light bulb would not work? He had over 9,000 failed attempts but kept trying until he reached his desired goal.

Today, we are all enjoying the benefits of this. He put everything at stake and acted in spite of uncertainties and kept trying until he got it. It's called life, many things, we may not get right the first time or the 20th time but if we don't give up and keep trying, we will eventually get it right.

Fear has prevented many dreams from being born but faith on the other hand has given birth to many extraordinary achievements by ordinary people.

You will never know how much power God has deposited in you if you don't starve your fear and feed your faith. Fear will put a limit on you and you will not reach the fullness of your potentials. Fear has torment, the

Bible says. It is possible to be so tormented by it that it can give way to physical illness in the body. It can take people out of life while they are still alive. It can keep people from stepping out in faith to explore new adventures and it sure can keep people from fulfilling God's purpose for their lives. Fear is a bondage, a trap of the enemy, it is not the plan of God for man at all.

Whatever you may be afraid of prior to picking up this book up and reading this chapter is just a false evidence appearing to be real. Don't yield your power to it, take it back, move forward in the opposite direction which is faith. Remember, without faith, it is impossible to please God. Faith can move mountains! Go forward by faith!

CHAPTER 11

HOW DO YOU SEE YOURSELF?

L IFE has a way of wanting to define us due to what we have been through. One thing I have found out is that, while you might have gone through some things, either good or bad, you must not allow those things to define who you are. It is true that some experiences may contribute to your perspective about life but how you see yourself and knowing who you are in God is what will eventually lead you to the fulfillment of your purpose in God.

So how should we see ourselves? The answer is simple; the way God sees us. You may be reading this book now and saying that, if only people knew what you have been through, they would understand why you have settled for where you are. I say, that is a limitation that circumstances might have put on you but you do not need to put it on yourself. You must determine to see yourself through the eyes of God and catch a glimpse of how He sees you.

I would like to talk about Gideon in the Bible. He was an Israelite who witnessed some hardship along with his people due to their disobedience to God. The Midianites attacked and terrorized the Israelites constantly, destroying their crops and livestock, leaving them no sustenance and putting them in fear. They huddled away from plain sights afraid of the Midianites and the other enemy countries that had joined in to terrorize them but they also cried out to God for help. **(Judges 6)**

It came to pass that, the Angel of the Lord appeared to Gideon and called out to him in a way that was the furthest from his mind. He said; **"The Lord is with you, you mighty man of valor."** **(Judges 6:12)** Of course, Gideon questioned that, simply because that was not how he saw himself. The Angel further surprised him by telling him to go in his "might" to fight the Midianites and Gideon thought it could not be possibly so. He might have even thought that, the Angel had the wrong person, he let the angel know that, his clan was the weakest in his tribe and he was the least in his father's house. You see how he defined himself?

This is exactly what many of us do to ourselves. When God looked down and saw Gideon, he saw a man he had put might and valor in, a man he had called to deliver his people from the hand of their oppressors. But when Gideon considered himself, he saw a weak man, from a weak clan and he himself being of no significance in that weak clan. All those things he stated had nothing to do with the way God saw him. He had an assignment, he had a definite purpose and he had been equipped for it so it was up to him to accept it and walk in the fullness of the power in him.

He wanted to make sure God was really sending him, he asked for some signs and it was after those things had been confirmed that he was fully convinced that God was truly sending him and he began to accept his assignment.

There is a giant within each and every one of us waiting to manifest God's glory but we must begin to see ourselves through the eyes of God not our background, circumstances and people's opinions of us.

God has equipped each and every one of us for whatever He has called us to do. The way He sees us is special and His

THE PLACE OF POWER IN YOU

acceptance is incomparable, His love is unconditional. He says, we are the apple of His eyes, He has our names written on the palm of His hands. He loved us so much He was willing to give His only Son as a ransom so that, He could gain us back to Himself.

If we can see ourselves the way He sees us, then we would fly high and soar like eagles. We would know that, there is nothing He is asking of us that He has not already given us the ability to carry out, we just need to manifest His glory.

I remember hearing the story of Les Brown many times, I wrote about him in one of the chapters of this book. He knew there was a gift in him but he battled within himself for years that he was not qualified because he was not college educated and the stage looked so big and seemed not to have room for non-college graduates. You see, that was his own perspective at the time and he allowed it to limit him from fulfilling God's calling upon His life. But when he finally rose up to it, he began to flow in the area of his gifting and today, the man is a gift to the world. His story is so touching and the odds he's had to overcome in his life are so compelling.

Until we begin to see ourselves the way God sees us rather than the way circumstances and people want to dictate to us, we may not really amount to anything. The way we see ourselves shows whether we accept our uniqueness and our calling or not.

The Christian Speaker and Author Joyce Meyer said that, when she told her friends, that she had the calling of God upon her life that God was going to use her and she would have the biggest women's ministry in the world, many did not believe it. She said in one of her sermons that, a friend actually had the gut to ask about this and when she answered affirmatively, the friend told her that "they" (she and the other friends) had thought about it and they did not think it (the vision Joyce had) was going to be possible due to her personality. Wow! How many times have people judged you based on one thing or the other in your life and put a lid on you? How many times have they written you off? That is up to them you know because God is singing a different tune about you.

I am glad to know that, Joyce Meyer stood steadfast in what she believed God was calling her to do, she went through her process and today, she has the biggest most impactful women's ministry in the world. This shows us clearly that, if the Lord is calling you out to do something, no one has the right to put a limitation on you and stop you, they can if you let them but if you see yourself the way God sees you and you embrace His gifts and callings upon your life, you will do exploits for Him.

Daniel was a slave in the land of Babylon but he had an extraordinary relationship with God, he saw himself as an Israelite whose forefather Abraham had a covenant with God. He remained in the reality of that knowledge and he would neither defile himself with the king's meat nor bow down to his idol, why? He knew whose he was. The result of all these, brought glory to his God and promotion to him and his friends. The way he saw himself was from the perspective of how God saw him, that alone turned the power in him on and he was able to overcome a lot of obstacles in the land of his captivity. He was taken in as a slave but he did not allow that to dominate him, he operated within the reality of the God he knew and served, that made him a force to be reckoned with.

It does not matter what your external circumstances may be at this time, you may even be facing some strong oppositions due to one thing or the other, do not buckle under that pressure, let faith and power surge from within you because it is there, if God lives in you, believe me it is there. Begin to see yourself the way God sees you, call yourself by the name He calls you not the name the world calls you.

If we would cultivate an intimate relationship with God, where we are in constant communication with Him, His love and acceptance will help us to see ourselves the way He sees us. We are His precious ones, He knows the number of hairs on our heads and He cares for us affectionately. This should give you confidence that, with Him on your side, you can move mountains.

I truly believe that, when you begin to see yourself the way God sees you and walk in the reality of that truth, things will begin to change from within you that will affect you and your outside environment. The aura you carry will be different, the ambience around you will be inviting, and people will be drawn to you because of that. The Bible says, *'we are the light of the world'* *(Matthew 5:14a)* and light shines everywhere even through the darkness.

Many critical and judgmental people are also very hard on themselves because they see everything through the lenses of their experiences. No wonder they say that, "hurt people also hurt others". if you have suffered rejection for so many times in your life, it is very easy to interpret even the most innocent actions as people rejecting you rather dealing with things objectively. The solution to that is to open your heart to be healed and let the effect of that healing flow into every area of your life, it will begin to change the way you respond to people and how you see things.

How about when you see yourself through your title? What of when that title is taken away, what will you do then? Yes! Titles do get taken away! CEO's do lose their jobs too, Businesses do fail and Owners do lose everything. Things happen and even Pastors lose their churches and ministries. What if everything they see about themselves is wrapped around these positions? You and I already know that, when that position goes, down goes their identity as well because they saw themselves through those lenses and that is a huge problem.

People find themselves in the field of hopelessness and despair due to the fact that, the way they have always seen themselves is attached to something in their lives and when that thing goes, there also goes their identity. It cannot be overemphasized; immersing yourself in your identity in Christ must be a lifestyle.

It is important for you to see yourself the way God sees you, if you don't know Him, it should make your heart so glad that, there is Someone who has accepted you no matter where you are in life, what you've done and who you are, Someone who has a definite purpose for your life so you are not a mistake. The realization of this should make you run to Him with everything you have and invite Him in. You cannot say you belong to Him if you have not received Him, this is what His word says; *(John 1:12; John 3:16)*

If you already know Him but you are not in that place where you see yourself the way God sees you, you have work to do. If you are willing to do that work, you will experience a life transformation. I will just list some things that can be helpful below, things that, I personally had to do in order to get to where I am able to see myself the way God sees me.

1. **KNOW** that, you are loved by God UNCONDITIONALLY. Many times, we think to ourselves that we know this but our actions do say otherwise. You cannot use works to earn God's love so stop striving, He loves you regardless. You may want to declare to yourself daily that, "GOD LOVES ME UNCONDITIONALLY" and let it sink into the deepest part of your being. *"You have been accepted in the Beloved"* the Scriptures say in *(Ephesians 1:6)*

2. **REJECT** every lie that you have believed about yourself. At this point, you may want to make a list of those
   things that constantly bombard your mind, trouble
   you and put these glasses of worthlessness on you. No
   Matter how tiny it may be, confront it. Things like; "No
   one likes me; I am too fat; I am stupid, I am too skinny;
   I am dumb; my family is too poor; I have no worth; I
   am not important to anyone; I don't have what it takes;
   people like me are not needed;" and so on. At this point,
   even you reading this book want me to stop because this
   list is too depressing but unfortunately, these are some
   of the types of lies people live with daily. Write your
   list, expunge these lies from your psyche, tear it up into
   shreds after you have written it, and flush it down the
   drain. And do this next thing.

3. **EMBRACE** what God says about you. Make another
   list of how you would have wanted to see yourself, how
   God sees you. Search the Scriptures about how God sees
   you, what He calls you, write them out or type them out.
   For example; **Psalm 139:14 says; "I am fearfully** and
   wonderfully made;" Deuteronomy 7:6 says; **"I am His
   treasured possession;" Psalm 17:8 says; "I am the
   apple of His eye."** I believe you want me to continue
   because these definitions are so comforting, so affirming.
   Get into action, declare this OUT LOUD to yourself
   every day until it enters your heart and overtake every
   negativity in there. Healing and deliverance will come I
   guarantee you that as someone, who has gone through
   and who continues to go through the same process.

4. **PUT UP** a fight within you. The fact that, you wrote
the list of those ugly thoughts and tore it up, flushing it
down the drain does not mean that, they will not try to
come back but now, you have to fight, in fact you fight
to maintain your stand about who God says you are not
what those thoughts say you are. The Bible says that,
"For the weapons of our warfare are not carnal but
mighty in God for pulling down strongholds, casting
down arguments and every high thing that exalts
itself against the knowledge of God, bringing every
thought into captivity to the obedience of Christ."
(2Corinthans 10:5).

You must pull down those strongholds. Strongholds are
hideouts for the devil, don't give room to him, send him
packing, and don't entertain him. There are times when
arguments go on in our heads, what are we to do? If
that argument is a lie, which means, if it does not line up
with how God sees you, cast it down! I love God! He has
given us the power and authority over every ability of the
enemy so if a thought, contrary to what God calls you
enters into your mind, take it captive and take authority
over it. It is work but if you must live victoriously, you
must put up this fight. You have already won!

5. **CATCH** a new vision. The way you see yourself
must change after having done the suggested previous
points. In your mind's eye, you must begin to see yourself differently. You must carry a new, positive and a
healthy picture of yourself. If truly you allow yourself
to embrace and accept what God says about you, there

is no way, you will not see a Bold you, a Healthy you, a
Happy you, a Beautiful you, a you that is going somewhere to happen. A you that knows that God has a plan
for him/her and you are not here by mistake. A you that
will excel in your careers and endeavors. A you that will
not only be blessed but be a blessing to others. A new
you must be visualized and that vision must become
a part of you, when it does, it will infiltrate every area
of your life. How you respond to things, how you treat
others, how you react to your present circumstances and
how you see your future. It will take a lot of spiritual,
emotional and mental work but you can get there.

The things I shared in this particular chapter are very personal
to me, I have been on a journey that has progressively propelled
me to where I am today. These points shared are so simple but
they work if taken seriously and applied diligently. We were made
in His image and we must see ourselves through those lenses.

CHAPTER 12

LIVE LIFE INTENTIONALLY

INTENTIONAL living is the way to go if you must achieve anything great in life. It is sad to say that, the word is spoken many times but not practiced. In order for you to awaken the giant within you, you have to take intentional steps, if not the giant will stay asleep.

It takes intentionality to respect yourself in the way you do things and respect others as well. It takes intentionality to treat others the way you want to be treated. It takes intentionality not to respond in negative ways to wrongs done to you but to take the high road, to forgive and release offenses extending grace. It takes intentionality to discipline yourself to rise up each day and make your day productive, to set goals and work hard at them to see that they come to pass.

I cannot over emphasize the benefits of intentional living. I myself became a student of intentionality in its full force some years ago. After having lived life the way it came to me and getting nothing from that experience but negativity and little joy. I decided that, it was time to start living life intentionally.

I quickly found out that, to live intentionally is to live life on purpose. It requires discipline, focused determination, sacrifices but it brings a great amount of joy and fulfillment not only to you but to everyone that you come in contact with. I believe that, the life that is centered only on oneself is not worth it, our lives must be able to glorify our Creator God and benefit humankind. We are naturally taken care of in the process. When you live a life of intentionality, you seek the highest good of other people. It is not about what you can get from them but what you can give them. Many times, giving is not only in form of money and material things, it can be as simple as a smile, a word of encouragement, affirming others, seeing them through the eyes of God, helping people out as much as it lies within your power.

It does not matter how life must have treated you in times past, you can rise up and intentionally make the best use of what you've got now. Living a life of intentionality is making the right choices and making a U-turn from a path that leads to destruction. For example, if a cycle is existing in your family lineage and it is a negative one, you do not have to let that cycle continue with you. With the help of God and making the right choices, you can break that cycle and chart a new course.

There were people who were raised by single parents not because the other parent was dead but because they just chose to stay out of their lives. Someone in this situation can pay attention to this and decide to do the exact opposite of what was done by being there for their own kids when they become a parent and by giving all the love and attention that they missed from their absentee parent.

Life is a journey and it must be intentionally handled. While there are many things that happen that are completely out of our control, there are many other things that are within our control as well. We choosing to do the right things even when it is hard to do or choosing the right attitude in a very challenging and difficult situation are all part of what we can control. I solidly believe that,

God has given unto each one of us the power to make the right choices if we so choose to do so.

There had been times in my life when I wished I had made better choices in the way I did things or responded to situations. There were times I had allowed my emotions to get the best of me rather than me keeping it under control so that it did not dominate me. At first, I used to think, well "this is the way God made me and I can't just help it" but I found out that, making such statements and believing them was a cup out for not wanting to change or do the right things.

In my on case, I began to really ask God for help in the areas I knew I needed change. It is important to say that, one of the ways, if not the best way you would know you have overcome a habit is when confronted with situations that challenge you to make a choice either good or bad alike.

Sometimes, when we pray this kind of prayer, one would wish that situations would just go away. It is not always like that, you would be faced with things that bring the real you out and that is the only time you can judge yourself and see if truly you have changed.

This was what began to happen to me as I asked for God's help and listened to the inner voice within me, helping me, guiding me to make the right choices, choose a better attitude. I would face situations literally designed to push "my button" only that, this time and period in my life, I am living intentionally, so instead of allowing my button to be pushed, I would take the high road, it is only by the grace of God. I must admit that, there would be times, my flesh would be "screaming" because it was used to reacting and I was not going to let it and it would get tired and shut up, I had won. It is not an easy road but it is a rewarding one, I am being changed daily through the grace of God.

I made up my mind to become a student of intentional living and become fully aware of my thoughts, words and actions with God's help backing me up and the rewards have been priceless.

I found out that, for the giant within me to fulfill God's plan, I must live my life intentionally but the good news is that, I don't have to do it in my own strength; God's grace is always available to anyone who would just ask.

Intentional living can spread to every area of our lives and relationships. If husband and wife would intentionally treat each other right, if parents would intentionally raise their kids pointing them in the right direction, if children would intentionally obey their parents who wholesomely parent them, if politicians would intentionally do what they are supposed to do, if a worker would intentionally give his or her best at work, if a leader would intentionally lead with the fear of God and not manipulate his/her followers, if people would intentionally treat one another the way they would want to personally be treated, our world would be a better place. But instead of looking at what everyone is doing or not doing, we can start with us.

If you get up each day setting at the start of your day to live life intentionally, tapping in to that power within you to do this, you will see significant changes in every area of your life. Sometimes, the price for intentional living seems too high for many people to pay and that is the reason why, our world is in the chaotic state it is right now. This human nature likes to be in charge and do what it likes without any sense of accountability but the result of it is the height of selfishness and lack of godly fear that this generation is experiencing.

People are constantly choosing evil over good, immorality over morality, many things are upside down, out of sync with the plan of God. In spite of all the mess going on in our world today,

we can still connect to the real Source of power which is God
Himself and let Him help us navigate our way through life, this
also takes being intentional.

CHAPTER 13

DREAM BIG.....DON'T HOLD BACK

I T is amazing to know that, God plants seeds of greatness in our hearts but He expects us to step in, take responsibility for the manifestation of it. So what happens if a person never does their part? It would never be God's fault. World renowned Speaker and Author, late Dr Myles Munroe said that, "the richest place on earth is the cemetery." Why? It is, because a lot of people are buried in the graves with their dreams and those dreams were never actualized.

Look around us and think for a moment, the chair you are sitting on, the book you are holding, the clothes on your body, they were all made out of something, they did not appear as finished products the first time, no! Some people somewhere creatively imagined how a tree can be cut down, goes through its process and be made into pieces of furniture and before you know it, you have a chair, a table, a cabinet and many other things. But what if, they just had the dream in their hearts and never got to work? There would be no furniture.

I strongly believe that, because the Creator lives on our inside, we also have the divine ability to create things. He has put a portion of Himself inside each and every one of us that, if we can discover it, we can have inventions upon inventions. Someone said; "there are many songs yet to be sung, many books yet to be written, many mysteries yet to be discovered." The onus lies on us to dig deep and discover what it is God has put on our inside and to actively work to bring it to life. Jim Rohn in one of his speeches said, "God asks us to plant a seed and He will make it a tree." There is our part and there is God's part, without the seed in the ground, there can be no tree but the good news is that, He has already put the seed within us. DREAM!

Many people are afraid to dream big because they do not really believe those dreams can come to pass. They cut themselves short and dream tiny dreams, they play safe through life. There is more to life than what it appears to be, we must be relentless in our quest to not only dream big but also accept the possibility that, dreams do come true...with a lot of hard work.

God has not called us to a mediocre life, throughout the Scriptures, He demonstrates how mighty things were done through ordinary people but it is sufficient to say that, they put their trust in God who was able to help them, they played a major part in stepping out in faith, they did not just sit, wishing things would happen, they obeyed, they acted and God showed up.

Abraham is a very popular man in the scriptures, he was called by God to leave his father's country and go to a land that the Lord would show Him. That was bold! To leave the familiar for the unfamiliar, the known for the unknown. Abraham was not called the father of faith for nothing, even though he had no idea where he was headed, he put his faith in God and trusted Him that, He was able to take care of him, his family and fulfill the promises He had given him. Coming to know God, if you don't know Him yet is like that, walking intimately with Him if you already know Him is like that. Many times, we want to see the full picture before we obey but all we have to do is get up and follow His lead by faith, one step at a time.

God put a dream in Abraham's heart, He told him that, he was going to be the father of many nations and by him all the nations of the earth would be blessed. **(Genesis 12)** This was the same Abraham who was childless but he believed God and carried the hope of that dream coming to pass in his heart. How do I know that? His name was Abram when God called him, Abram means "high father" in Hebrew but God later renamed him and called him Abraham which means "father of a multitude". Imagine he was childless but he went about telling everyone something like this; "my name is no longer Abram but Abraham, God told me I would be the father of many nations." He must have been mocked, talked about and insulted even, maybe some people called him a joker or a dreamer. He did not allow all of these things to bother him, he held on steadfastly to the promise that was given to him and it came to pass. Today, thousands of years after he has passed on, his seed remains upon the earth and everyone that comes to put their trust in God becomes a seed of Abraham and partake of the blessings that God bestowed on him when he cut covenant with him. That dream came to pass; he was and is indeed the father of a multitude.

The dream in your heart may be bigger than you and you know it would take more than what you know and have to bring it to pass. That is a God given dream, don't run away from it, embrace it, trust God and work hard, you will experience things that, human mind cannot fully comprehend. Generations after generations have passed, the human mind can still not explain how a ninety year old Sarah (Abraham's wife) conceived and became a mother or how a virgin conceived and gave birth to our Lord and Savior. The ways of God are unsearchable, His wisdom is infinite, what He purposes to do, He will do but you must play your part. What if Abraham refused to obey God or Mary rejected the unheard of idea of being pregnant without knowing a man? Think for a minute.

When you really look at it, if God has put a dream in your heart, it will glorify Him and bless others and in the process, your life will be greatly fulfilled. We miss the mark many times because we think it is about us and we turn the attention to self rather than God.

For people who do not know the Lord, there is a vacuum in the heart of every human being that, no one or thing can fill, only God can fill it. When an individual accepts Him, He makes our heart His home and if we allow Him, He will show us great and mighty things that we do not know according to the Holy Scriptures.

Imagine knowing Him and being able to talk to Him about the dreams that, He puts in your heart, how exciting is that? He will show you how to go about fulfilling it, He will back you up and pick you up when you fall, He will hold your hand and you will never be alone.

I carried a dream of becoming an author in my heart for as long I can remember, I have trusted Him along the way even when I did not know where and how to start but when the time was ripe and I kicked into action, He began to make things happen by Himself, connecting me with the right people to help me along the way. He has brought this book into your hand right now by divine design and my sincere prayer is that, after having read this book, your soul will be ignited in some form to dream big and follow your own dreams knowing fully well that, the power to do so is already within you.

I always knew that my words came to me easily and I was not

afraid or shy to stand in front of people to speak, many times I do not have to premeditate, God just fills my mouth with words to say on the platforms He gives me, I knew I was called to be a Speaker that brings hope and awakening to people. I would see myself on stages ever before I had my first opportunity to speak and a passion that I can't put into words would exude from me, I continue to carry this dream in my heart and continue to trust God as I step out in boldness to do what I have been called to do fully. The fulfilling part comes when I feel deep within me that, I have represented God well and when people testify about being touched and blessed as a result. Words will never be able to adequately describe the feelings of humility and gratitude that overtake my being at such moments.

It is not because I am better than anyone but over the years, in the course of my walk with God, the love relationship that God and I have and the processes He has taken me and continues to take me through, I know that, He is true to His promises, He will do what He has promised to do, if I will do my part, He is faithful to do His.

I want to challenge you to embrace your God given dreams, whatever it may be. It can be as simple as starting a new business, a ministry, going on a mission field, inventing an idea that has been put in your heart, run towards your dreams and embrace them tightly. If you know the Lord, trust in Him every step of the way and do not lean on your own understanding, acknowledge Him in all your ways and He will direct your path, so says His word **(Proverbs 3:5-6).** If you do not know Him, I appeal to you to open your heart and invite Him in, He is real and He is knocking on the door of your heart. This book did not get to your hand by accident, He is using it as a tool to draw you to Him. Let Him in and your life will never be the same again.

Our world is constantly changing, new things are appearing every single day. New inventions, better working models of several machines. There was a time when a Television set was so bulky and heavy with an extended rear, some people thought of a better way to package it and boom! We have flat screen televisions everywhere. There was a time when flip phones reigned but now, we have more advanced cell phones with many features more than we can even handle. I believe it all began with dreams in the hearts of individuals, dreams they followed through with that became realities.

Whatever has been put in your heart, you have been appointed for that assignment, rise up and work diligently on it, even when you make mistakes, don't give up. It may be hard sometimes, there will be bumps along the way, it's okay, it's all part of the process, don't quit on it, keep going, hold on to God's unchanging hands and you will reap the fruits, God will get the glory and humanity will be blessed.

No one can dream your dream, only you can. Don't let fear stop you, don't let circumstances stop you, don't let people stop you and don't stop yourself.

There are few points you may want to consider to get you thinking about your dreams.

1. **WRITE**

   What are the ideas popping up in your heart? Write them down, keep a journal and write them down. *Habakkuk 2:2* says that; *"Write the vision and make it plain on tablets, that he may run who reads it."*

2. PRAY AND BELIEVE

It sounds so simple but if you don't believe that your
dream will come to pass, the probability that it will is
very slim. Cover it in prayer and stay in faith believing.
Mark 11:24 says that; *"Whatever things you ask when
you pray, believe that you receive them and you will
have them."*

3. TRUST IN THE LORD

If you did not know the Lord by the time you started
reading this book, it is my sincere hope that, by now your
heart is open to receive Him. For your dreams to come
to pass, trusting the Lord will make your way easier and
help your process to be meaningful. There is a divine
satisfaction that comes with trusting the Lord. If you
already know Him, be reassured that, He wants to see
those dreams come to pass, trust in Him all the way.
**Proverbs 3:5-6 says; Trust in the Lord with all your
heart, and lean not on your own understanding; in
all your ways acknowledge Him, and He will direct
your paths."**

4. WORK HARD

Like I said earlier on, you have a responsibility to see
your dream become a reality, you have a part to play in
the journey. Whatever your dream is, work hard at it, do
research on it, educate yourself, learn all you can and
seek wise counsel. Any dream with no activity is just a
wishful thinking. **Proverbs 14:23 says; "In all labor
there is profit, but idle chatter leads only to poverty."**

5. DON'T STOP

Even when the journey becomes difficult, don't quit, keep forging ahead, stand strong and go on. Surround yourself with people who believe in you and your dreams, people who can positively speak into your life so that, when the going gets tough, you have some sweetness flowing back to you. It is priceless to have a circle of people who will support you through thick and thin.

Dreams are freely given to us by God, don't run away from them, dream and do it BIG because God is BIG!

CHAPTER 14

THE WORLD IS WAITING FOR YOU

DO you know that, you were made for a purpose? You are not here by accident or by mistake. Regardless of where you have come from or been through, there is something unique about you that the Creator packaged in your DNA and only you can bring that forth. What if you fail to do so? You would be robbing your generation of the privilege of getting to know the unique you and the abilities within you.

Life happens and robs many of their confidence, self-esteem and self-worth. Their dreams become dead and their vision becomes dulled. They can't see beyond now and that's all there is about them. But life is much more than going to work, earning a paycheck and just paying bills. Life is about fulfilling our God given purpose, living our God given dreams, glorifying Him and impacting humanity.

To some people this may sound like Greek because when they look around them, all they see is nothingness and in that, there is no excitement about life. The Bible says that; *"My people perish for lack of knowledge" (Hosea 4:6).* What if we all come to the realization of the knowledge that, we were made for a purpose? Many people's lives will have a new meaning. The way they live their lives will change, how they view their future will be different, there will be a stirring on their inside, steps will be taken, goals will be set and races will be run. That is exactly what I am trying to achieve with this chapter and this book in its entirety.

You were divinely designed by God to carry out an assignment here on earth. When you look around, there are many people with special abilities that you probably do not possess and that is okay. They were designed for that, hopefully they are using it for God's glory and blessing humanity in the process.

There are people with the ability to; sing, speak, design, organize, invent, coordinate and so on and so forth. You will see people who are very good with their hands; they can dismantle an equipment and assemble it with ease, while some of us spend a good amount of time trying to figure out how to turn that equipment on or off. That is what they have been gifted to do. The builders build, what if there were no builders to build, we would all be living in an open space or something. Some love to cook, they can whip ingredients together and come out with a mouthwatering dish. Many of these people also love what they do. While some people learn how to do it, for some people, it is their inherent ability.

The beautiful aspect of this is that, God has designed everyone to contribute something to the universe and it is something that someone else will need and make use of. I can't make a car but I sure need one. I can't build a house but I do live in one. What that tells me is that, there is something unique in you and me that this world needs and it is our responsibility not only to discover it but to work on and master it in order to bless humanity and glorify God with it.

The world is waiting for you to sing your song, write your books, preach your sermon, invent the latest, something within you is to be given expression to and no one can do that but you.

You may say, well I don't know what my purpose is? Don't sit around just wondering about it, talk to your Maker and try your hands on something you are drawn to and give it a shot. It does not hurt to try something, if it doesn't feel right after trying, you can try something else until you know exactly what you are meant to do. You can also discover your gifting or purpose in the process of doing something else.

Several years ago, I got involved in a direct selling business and I had to talk to people all the time, before the business, I was a stay-at-home mom trying to figure out what to do. In the process of doing the business, I advanced and moved up the career ladder as a Director, that created a platform for me to coach people directly and speak at events regularly. I knew I had the natural God given ability to speak but I must say that, doing this business brought it out of me full force, now it was no longer just me that recognized the gift, others began to see it and be blessed by it and I could not be more amazed by how God worked things out.

Remember, I did not want to do the business or any business at all in the first place as I mentioned in an earlier chapter because I did not consider myself a sales person neither did I like sales. However, I needed to not sit around waiting for a huge miracle to happen, I had to try my hands on what was in front of me which was this business and since then, many other things including what I now consider God's calling upon my life have come to light. I am forever grateful for that opportunity. The business became a stepping stone for me to greater heights.

I told the story above to let you know that, in case you are still in a place where you don't know what you've been called to do or you know it but don't know how to go about it, I encourage you not to wait any longer, find something to do and do it with all diligence. *(Ecclesiastes 9:10)*.

When you know what you are meant to do, there is a joy that

comes with that, for every prize, there is a price, and you must work at it until you get good at it. It is the area of your strength that, if you apply disciplined effort at, you can come out the best.

I have heard this before in many ways but Joyce Meyer simply puts it in one of her sermons that, if you are a 7 at something, if you work diligently at it, you can become a 9 or even a 10. The world is looking for 10's. But if you are a 4 at something, you can work hard and become a 7. Don't forget that, the world is looking for 10's, the world needs 10's so why don't you find out what you are good at and work very hard at it to become the best you can be. Everyone is drawn to quality, they will be drawn to you when you work hard on yourself.

If someone has a gift of music and they go to music school to learn how to read music, play instruments and really get good at that gift, they practice for endless hours getting good at their art, they will surely be sought after.

The Almighty God gave us our gifts, talents and abilities for a purpose. My son is 8 years old right now and he draws cartoons all the time, I look at his writings, his sense of imagination and I know without any doubt that, it was given to him by God, no one coached him to do that. If he goes to write stories that can be a blessing to his generation, encouraging little kids like him to be kind to others, advising them to develop healthy habits and telling them about the love of Jesus Christ, not only will he be fulfilling a purpose, He will be glorifying God and blessing humanity in the process. There are many books out there that draw people to destruction, we all sure can use some helpful books especially the young generation so if my son develops his gift, there is already a place in this world for it.

I have made it a priority in my life to affirm people and point out the special abilities they may possess, peradventure this may help someone discover God's purpose for their life. I remember talking to a friend of mine who was really contemplating about starting her own law firm, she loves her career, she is honest and has a lot to offer families in her practice without taking advantage of them like many people do. I am glad to say that, she was able to step out in faith and she has a blossoming practice now blessing people and connecting them with God in the process. Sometimes, people need that affirmation, they need others to believe in them. Don't wait until someone affirms you, go ahead and affirm others, show your support and belief in them, before you know it, the seeds of kindness that you sow will start coming back to you in bountiful harvest.

Dealing with moving companies here in America can be quite frustrating, having moved around quite a bit, we have dealt with a number of fraudulent people. It was just so refreshing to find out that, one of our good friends started a moving company and their main goal is to offer business with integrity which many are not doing in that industry. What Curtis Isaac is doing with his Muviture company is so encouraging and I have no doubt that, his vision was born in him with a purpose behind it. You see, the world needs people like that.

What can you bring to the table of life? You have something within you right now that the world needs. You can either discover it and dream away without working on it and all it would be is a wishful thinking or you can discover it, cooperate with God and go to work, be the best you can be, glorifying God and blessing everyone that comes in contact with you in the process.

God has awesome plans for us and when we walk with Him, He will bring us to that glorious future He has for us. He says in **Jeremiah 29:11; "For I know the thoughts that I think toward you, says the Lord, thoughts of peace and not of evil, to give**

you a future and a hope." It starts by accepting Christ into our hearts as our Lord and Savior and walking intimately with God every step of the way. He will lead and guide you if you let Him.

I want to enjoy what God has prepared for me, not only in heaven but here on earth as well. I want to fulfill His purpose, bringing Him glory and reconnecting people back to Him. The world is waiting for the manifestations of God's children so don't waste another minute or day wondering around in the field of life. Ask your Maker right now to put you on the path He has designed for you, seize the opportunities that He brings your way because THE WORLD IS WAITING FOR YOU!

CHAPTER 15

YES! YOU CAN DO IT

IT may be that, you have discovered your purpose, or caught a glimpse of the future and you are wondering how can it be? It couldn't possibly be true! Why? You've seen something glorious, amazing and unbelievably magical and you can't simply comprehend how you would end up in that arena of life doing the things that your mind's eye has just perceived. Wait a minute! Before you write yourself off, take a deep breath and declare that, you can do it.

If you see what you can achieve, then it is easy to go about it and achieve it but if you see something bigger than you then you know you need Someone bigger than you to bring it to pass through you. You do not need to worry, you just need to cooperate with God and let Him guide you through it but know that, you can do it.

Yes it will take a lot of sacrifice, it will take determination and painful effort but you can get to that future that God has for you. That dream in your heart can come to pass. We were made for greatness, we were made to fulfill a purpose, out of the billions of people on earth, each one of us has been designed uniquely. Even twins that share the same womb for nine months and come into this world on the same day have their own unique purposes in God.

There is nothing that is being asked of you that you have not yet been equipped to do. It will take some digging deep within to fetch the treasures out. One of the chapters of this book talks about process, yes you will go through a process but you can do it. Whatever you were meant to do, you were created for and you can do it, the power to do it is already in you.

Many times people would rather not even go near anything that challenges their thinking because they can't see how it can become possible. They are filled with so much negativity that has fed their mind with information of a low life, low self-image and low self- worth never amounting to anything that, they can't visualize anything outside of the box of their misery.

Yet, the fact that, we were made for a purpose does not mean that, things will drop on us like ripe a cherry. In order to do what we have been called to do, we must run towards it. I am not trying to demonstrate any form of spookiness when I talk about God being the ultimate Helper that can get us to achieving that purpose. I like what He says in **Psalm 32:8; "I *will instruct you and teach you in the way you should go; I will guide you with my eye"*.** What a comfort! What a joy to know that, in this journey of life, we can never be without direction if we just follow hard after Him.

I have seen many people wander about with no direction when they should have gone into the Owner's manual which is the Word of God. In it, I find answers to everything and I mean every solution to any situation in life is in the Owner's manual. Yes! He is a big God but He is also willing to reach us at the level where we are to help us navigate our way through life.

God tells us in His word; *"Fear not, for I am with you; Be not dismayed, for I am your God. I will strengthen you, Yes, I will help you, I will uphold you with my righteous right hand.'* *(Isaiah 41:10)* Just meditating on scriptures like this alone energizes me from within. When there is a task in front of me to be done, a goal to achieve or a dream to actualize and fear grips my heart, telling me that, it can't be done, I go into my Owner's Manual and immerse myself in His word like the one I just quoted, I allow it to take over the fear that I feel and I just move forward in faith. It sounds too easy you may say but what I love about God is that, His ways are simple. His word is not just ink on paper, it is powerful, alive and life transforming.

I remember counseling with a young lady who was trying to finish college and graduate but she was finding a particular subject very hard and she was saying it. Of course, what you say long enough becomes the picture you see. She had asked me to pray with her but instead, I counseled her because you see, it does not do her any good if I prayed for or with her and the picture she saw through the confession of her mouth still remained the same. I encouraged her to change her words regarding the subject and begin to declare what she would like to see, to say words like "I like Math, I understand it because I have the mind of Christ, the Holy Spirit teaches me and I excel" and so on and so forth. She should also give herself to diligent study of the course. With her words, she began to change the picture she saw, before long, it took root in her heart and began to change her attitude towards the subject, with that, came the open mind to receive what was being taught and the desire to review and study, with that came understanding and illumination. In the end she passed the course in flying colors. Nothing changed about the course but something had to change on her inside for the outside to change. She could do it, she could absolutely excel, she just had to change her attitude and her words.

Regardless of what goals you have set or the vision you have seen, you can reach your desired destination, you can do it. Maybe you do not even have a goal because you are too afraid of failing, you are afraid of being embarrassed and disappointed and you have built a wall around you so thick that nothing can penetrate, believe me, the only person losing the most is you. If you must admit, you may temporarily guard yourself against some things but ultimately, you are allowing yourself and others to be cheated. Cheated of the experience of the divine abilities within you and you are cheating others from witnessing the manifestation of those divine abilities.

Fear is one thing that stops people from stepping out in faith and I have touched on that in a previous chapter of this book. Don't give in to fear because if you do, you will just be a wondering generality instead of a meaningful specific as rightly stated by Zig Ziglar.

Poor self- image sometimes makes people think they can't do what they have been called to do or what they have set their heart to do. They wrongly believe that, it is okay for others to achieve greatness but not them but hey! God never created anyone to be a second class citizen, as far as He is concerned, we all have equal opportunities and equal chances at this game of life. Are you willing to play? Get rid of poor self -image, again, there are chapters in this book that do touch on that. Begin to see yourself as God sees you, you are a mountain mover! That is what He says.

Here are some tips that can help you along the way;

1. **CREATE THE PICTURE**

    Some people create goal posters, I have one too. There is power in visualizing the end result of a dream. It creates a why, that why gives you the energy to run towards your goal every day.

2. **BE DETERMINED**

    You must be prepared to face obstacles along the way,

it is called life. There will be bumps on this journey but you must be determined not to quit prematurely. God's strength is made perfect in our weakness the word of God says. Lean on God's strength all the way because yours can only take you so far but His is limitless and has no end.

3. **SPEAK LIFE**

No matter how hard it gets, refuse to speak negatively, speak the word of life at all times. You may say that is hard to keep up with, I agree that, it will take some discipline but it can be done. I have found out that, whatever you give voice to becomes bigger, if you give voice to a negative situation, you are giving it gas to run but if you speak life and declare what you expect to see, sooner or later, you will begin to see the results.

I remember that when I started the business I talked about in one of the chapters, it was in a city where I did not know anyone and it involved doing things with people, which meant I had to approach strangers. There was just no other option for me than to get out there and talk to people I did not know. I had to do it even though I must admit, I was really nervous but one thing that helped me so much was the affirmation I began to declare upon myself every day before I stepped out. I would say things like "I am a booking machine; people love me; they want to do business with me; the favor of God is upon me; people are drawn to me," and so on so forth. Yes initially, I got many no's but I stuck to my affirmation and kept working and it got to a point where things changed and I began to get great results. I am a firm Believer that, when we say the mind of God concerning us, and we stick to it no matter what, we will see results.

4. RUN TOWARDS IT AND PAY THE PRICE

What is your dream? What is your goal? What is that call upon your life? Run towards it, go in the direction God will take you. Many times, He may take you through unfamiliar territories, it is not to harm you but it is to mold you into the champion He has called you to be. Like I said in a previous chapter, Joseph's dream was to rule but even as he ran towards it in belief, God took him through the pit, Potiphar's house, prison and ultimately to the Palace.

The person who has a dream of losing weight will go through some serious discomfort while working out but when the desired weight is achieved, all the painful exercises will be worth it.

When I began to run towards the call of God upon my life and I had to give up a lot of things, one major one was spending hours in front of the T.V. so that, I could spend more hours in prayer and study. At first, it was hard because I was used to it but as time went on and on, it became easier to the point that, now I go weeks without watching it and I don't miss it. I am able to get a lot of things done because I have freed some time from watching the TV.

In your case, you may have to go to school and educate
yourself more, you may have to under study someone or
submit yourself under some form of authority to serve
and be mentored. There will be prices to be paid but in
the end, the joy that comes with the reward is undeniable
and cannot be adequately put into words.

5. **SURROUND YOURSELF, BE ACCOUNTABLE**
    There is a saying that, you will be like the five closest
    people in your life. Who are those people in your own
    life right now? Do they believe in you and the purpose
    of God for your life? Do they add value to you or
    subtract from the one you have? Do they constructively
    correct you or destructively put you down? Are they
    people you can trust to be accountable to or you would
    rather hide from them? These are some of the ques-
    tions you want to ask yourself when you are surrounding
    yourself with people and asking them to hold you
    accountable. It is important to have coaches and
    mentors who help you and can see things from a healthy
    perspective.

6. **ABOVE ALL...TRUST GOD**
    I cannot over emphasize the power of placing your trust
    in God and allowing Him to walk this journey with you.
    David who was one of the most powerful men to ever
    live, till today, the story of David killing the giant Goliath
    still resonates, this same David was bragging about
    walking with God in **Psalm 18:29 saying, "With Your
    help I can advance against a troop; with my God I
    can scale a wall."** With God on your side, helping you

along the way, you can do anything. Even when things get tough, He will make it work out for your good. It does not mean that because you are trusting Him, everything will be trouble free but you can be sure of victory at the end of it all.

It is my sincere prayer that, every content of every chapter of this book in one way or another adds value to you and helps you in your journey. I pray that, you are able to manifest your better original self, bringing glory to God and being a blessing to your generation!

"Now to Him who is able to do exceedingly above all we ask or think, according to the power that works in us, to Him be glory in the Church by Christ Jesus to all generations, forever and ever. amen."

- Ephesians 3:20-21

TO CONTACT THE AUTHOR

Your prayer requests are welcomed. Please go to www.push-prayer.org and fill out a prayer request page. Prayer team attends to every request.

To invite Toyin to speak at your events, you may contact her at www.toyinjohn.com.

You may follow Toyin John on: Twitter, Instagram, Facebook, Periscope and LinkedIn. You may also subscribe to her Youtube Channel for inspirational messages.

Toyin and her prayer team hold weekly prayer conference call every Saturday at 8am eastern. Check out the Prayer ministry website at www.pushprayer.org for details.

Toyin is a Certified Speaker, Coach and Trainer with the John Maxwell team, she finds joy in coaching organizations as well as individuals to reach their peak performance. To contact her for group or one-on-one coaching services please do so at www.toyinjohn.com.

Internet addresses:
www.toyinjohn.com
www.giantwithin.org
www.pushprayer.org